The Royal Canadian Mounted Police 1873-1987

Text by DAVID ROSS
Military Curator, Parks Canada

and ROBIN MAY

Colour Plates by RICHARD HOOK

D1509223

OSPREY PUBLISHING LONDON

Published in 1988 by
Osprey Publishing Ltd
Member company of the George Philip Group
12–14 Long Acre, London WC2E 9LP
© Copyright 1988 Osprey Publishing Ltd

British Library Cataloguing in Publication Data

Ross, David
    Royal Canadian Mounted Police.—
    (Men-at-arms series; 197).
    1. Royal Canadian Mounted Police
    I. Title   II. May, Robin   III. Series
    363.2′0971   HV8157

    ISBN 0-85045-834-X

Filmset in Great Britain
Printed through Bookbuilders Ltd, Hong Kong

Acknowledgements
This book relies heavily on the research and
published work of the RCMP Historian, Dr. S. W.
Horrall, to whom sincere thanks are due. The
assistance of the Director of the RCMP Centennial
Museum, Mr. Malcom Wake has been invaluable
over many years. The help and support of Parks
Canada; the Glenbow Museum; Brig.Gen. J. L.
Summers, CMM, MC, CD (Ret'd), Mr. H. M. Garrett
and Staff Sgt. David Church is gratefully
acknowledged, as is our debt to the authors of all the
books listed in the bibliography.

Dedication
This book is dedicated to the memory of all the
Members of the Force who have died in the
performance of their duty in peace and war.

Artist's Note
Readers may care to note that the original paintings
from which the colour plates in this book were
prepared are available for private sale. All
reproduction copyright whatsoever is retained by the
publisher. All enquiries should be addressed to:
    Scorpio Gallery
    50 High Street,
    Battle,
    Sussex TN33 0EN
The publishers regret that they can enter into no
correspondence upon this matter.

Introduction

The Royal Canadian Mounted Police is the national police force of Canada; Canada is a federal state, however, and certain police powers are controlled by the provinces and the municipalities.

Canada is divided into two territories under the direct jurisdiction of the federal government, and ten provinces each with its own separate elected legislature, premier and cabinet. Law enforcement in each province is the responsibility of the provincial Attorney General. Most provinces at one time or another have had their own provincial police forces; today only the largest, Quebec and Ontario, recruit and administer their own forces. The other provinces contract with the RCMP to provide police services, under the direction of their Attorney Generals. In addition, all major cities and many smaller towns have their own municipal police forces. The two territories—the Yukon and the North-West Territories—are policed by the RCMP under federal jurisdiction.

This is a simplified explanation of a very complex web of relationships and legal responsibilities. There are numerous exceptions, anomalies and variations within this general picture, but it does illustrate the strong Canadian desire to have localised rather than central control of law enforcement.

It is obvious that this apparently cumbersome system would not work without a great measure of goodwill and close co-operation between law enforcement agencies throughout the country, nor would it be accepted without numerous legislated checks on the arbitrary use of police powers by individual policemen or their political masters.

The Commissioner of the RCMP, who is always a career officer of the Force, might be thought to hold a position of great power as the head of the national police force. However, he is a completely

Capt. (local Lt.Col.) George Arthur French, CMG, Royal Artillery, Commissioner of the North West Mounted Police 1873–76, wearing full dress Imperial Army Staff tunic. French had served in Canada 1862–66 with the British garrison, and as Inspector of Artillery, Canadian Militia, 1870–73. His administrative and logistical skills were a major factor in the success of the 'March West' in 1874; but clashes with his political masters in Ottawa led to his enforced resignation in 1876. He resumed his military career, serving in England, Australia and India before retiring in 1902 as Maj.Gen. Sir Arthur French. (RCMP)

non-political figure, highly respected professionally, reporting to the federal Solicitor General, a relatively junior cabinet minister. For a number of years now the term of appointment of the Commissioner has been set at three years.

Although the Mounted Police has many military-style traditions (and until 1900 even possessed some rather inadequate artillery), it is not a para-military body: it does not possess such equipment as armoured vehicles. Nor, since 1984, has it operated the national intelligence and counter-intelligence agency, a function it originally took over in 1920.

Founded in 1873 as the North West Mounted Police (NWMP), the Force became the Royal North West Mounted Police (RNWMP) in 1904 and the Royal Canadian Mounted Police (RCMP) in 1920. In keeping with the bilingual nature of Canada's federal government services it is today the Royal Canadian Mounted Police/Gendarmerie Royale du Canada (RCMP/GRC).

All ranks from commissioner to constable are known as 'Members', and many specialist support services are provided by 'Civilian Members' and federal public servants. Today the RCMP has 18,000 members and a budget of more than $1 billion with which to enforce federal laws covering such areas as drug enforcement, the criminal code, economic crime (tax evasion, counterfeiting, computer crime etc.), import and export regulations, illegal immigration, and even the migratory birds convention, in addition to a strong emphasis on preventive policing through community co-operation, electronic data processing security, and protection of government and foreign embassy personnel and property. The RCMP also operates forensic laboratories, the national fingerprint inventory and the Canadian Police College. The Force has more than 6,000 transport vehicles, including 29 aircraft, a large variety of boats and

Earliest known photograph of the North West Mounted Police, probably taken in 1874. All ranks wear the scarlet Norfolk jacket supplied from Militia stores. Officers had a gold Austrian knot on the cuff and, in common with senior NCOs, a gold band on the pillbox cap; other ranks had white cap-bands. Trousers had double white seam stripes. The puggaree, right, was soon discarded. Seated is Sub.Insp. John French, brother of the Commissioner, killed at Batoche in 1885; behind him, with sidewhiskers, is Sub-Insp. Francis Dickens, son of the novelist Charles Dickens. (RCMP)

over 50 horses for the Musical Ride and ceremonial escorts.

The Force operates its own training facility at the Depot in Regina, Saskatchewan, which trains nearly 300 recruits a year as well as providing advanced career courses, and one of the best specialised museums in Canada, the RCMP Centennial Museum. Competition for employment in the RCMP is intense, and the Force is able to pick and choose from the best of those seeking a law enforcement career.

The Beginnings

Since 1670, when Charles II granted a charter to the Governor and Company of Adventurers of England trading into Hudson's Bay, western North America—including what are now the states of Washington and Oregon—was ruled by this commercial company, better known today as the Hudson's Bay Company. The company's staple business was trading in furs obtained from the native people, so it was naturally in the 'adventurers'' interests to retain the country as a great game preserve. Attempts at settlement were largely discouraged, though the Red River colony grew up on the site of the present city of Winnipeg, and Upper and Lower Fort Garry were constructed as HBC headquarters and entrepôt facilities.

With the establishment of the Dominion of Canada in 1867 the control of more than half the country by a commercial company became an awkward anomaly, and steps were taken to transfer to the Crown Rupert's Land, (named after Prince Rupert, cousin of Charles II). The transfer was ineptly handled by the government, who failed adequately to consult with the Indians, the *Metis* (mixed bloods), the white traders and the hunters of the area, all of whom felt—with much justification—that their traditional and partly nomadic way of life was being threatened. The lack of insight and sympathy shown by the federal government formed at Confederation created general mistrust amongst the local inhabitants, and considerable unrest developed.

Louis Riel came forward as the leader of the dissident *Metis*; he established a Provisional

Suppression of the illegal whiskey trade was a principal duty of the NWMP on its arrival in the West. *'First Whiskey Spilled'*, a water-colour sketch by Assistant Surgeon Richard Barrington Nevitt, shows the destruction of confiscated liquor, *c.*1874. Now in the Glenbow Museum, Calgary, this picture from Nevitt's sketchbook is the earliest record of the colour of NWMP uniforms: shirts are shades of grey-blue, breeches tan, russet or grey.

Government of Rupert's Land and the North-West, and sought to negotiate with the federal government. The government, however, treated the movement as rebellion, and dispatched the Red River Expedition under the command of Col. Garnet Wolseley to re-establish Canadian control. The expedition, which was a logistical masterpiece, consisted of two specially raised militia battalions, the Quebec and Ontario Rifles, and the 2nd Battalion of the 60th King's Royal Rifle Corps. The rebellion collapsed almost without bloodshed, and Riel fled into exile in the United States. A provisional battalion of militia was left at Red River to maintain order. A number of future Mounted Police officers (including James Macleod, Sam Steele, A. G. Irvine and Charles Constantine) served on the expedition and in the provisional battalion.

To restore order in the districts surrounding Fort Garry, a small mounted police force was organised from the men of the provisional battalion and placed under command of Capt. Villiers of the Quebec Battalion of Rifles. This small group was the first police force to be organised in western Canada.

No sooner had the Manitoba crisis subsided when, in 1871 and 1872, alarming reports of restlessness among the Indians of the North-West came to the attention of the Canadian Parliament.

Having seen the advance of settlement in the western United States, the Indians were concerned about the fate of their traditional lands in Canada. An influx of traders dealing in cheap whiskey was also creating problems. There were reports of battles between rival tribes of Indians, and between Indians and traders. Indian fears were greatly increased by the cold-blooded massacre of a band of Assiniboines by white traders in the Cypress Hills in 1873.

Peace and order were vital if settlers were to be attracted to open up the Western Plains. It was also of paramount importance to establish Canadian sovereignty in the area to forestall the possibility of American expansion. By the international conventions of the day, land could be claimed by symbolically planting the flag, but the claim had to be made good by establishing a government presence to administer justice, postal services, land registry and customs posts, etc.

The Mounted Police, partly by accident and partly by design, were an ideal instrument to consolidate Canada's claims. By forcing the retreat of the whiskey traders and by prosecuting the perpetrators of the Cypress Hills Massacre, they effectively demonstrated that Canadian laws were to be observed and obeyed. Before long the Mounted Police collected customs duties, ran a mail service and carried out economically the duties of other departments—a boon to a government chronically short of revenue. In effect, the Police became the government of much of the Prairies. The dangers inherent in combining the rôles of police, judge, jury and gaoler were largely avoided due to the pragmatic and paternalistic outlook of the officers in command and the desire of both the Indians and the settlers for a stable and law-abiding climate.

The Creation of the Force

The idea of a mounted police force had germinated in the mind of the Prime Minister, Sir John A. Macdonald, backed up by two on-the-spot reports at his disposal. In the autumn of 1870 Lt. W. F. Butler (later Gen. Sir William), an officer of the British Army, had been commissioned to journey through the North Saskatchewan River area to determine the situation among the Indians and settlers. Butler completed a trip of more than 1,000 miles in the dead of winter. Among other things, he recommended the establishment of a 'well-equipped force from 100 to 150 men, one-third to be mounted', for the purpose of policing the North-West.

James Farquharson Macleod, CMG, second Commissioner of the NWMP, in undress uniform, March 1879: dark blue pillbox, scarlet tunic and blue breeches. A handsome man of considerable charm, Macleod was widely trusted by the Indians, whose plight in the face of advancing white settlement he tried to alleviate. A lawyer, he joined the Militia in 1856, and served as Brigade Major on Wolseley's Red River expedition of 1870. Appointed Assistant Commissioner in 1874, he succeeded French as Commissioner in 1876. He resigned in 1880 due to a clash with the Prime Minister over the rising costs of the Force, and became Stipendiary Magistrate of the North West Territories. (Topley photograph, Glenbow Museum)

In 1872 Lt.Col. P. Robertson-Ross, Adjutant-General of the Canadian Militia, was dispatched by the Canadian Government into the North-West on a fact-finding journey. He recommended the posting of one regiment of mounted riflemen, 550 strong, in the North-West.

On 3 May 1873 Sir John A. Macdonald introduced a bill respecting the administration of justice and for the establishment of a police force in the North-West Territories. On 23 May the bill was passed, and, on Royal Assent, the North-West Mounted Police came into being.

The original intention was to provide a force organised on military lines, not to exceed 300 men, under the command of a commissioner and assisted by a number of superintendents. In September 1873, it was decided to mobilise three divisions of 50 men each at Fort Garry, Manitoba. Pending the appointment of a commissioner, the men reported to Lt.Col. Osborne Smith, Deputy Adjutant-General of the Militia, at Fort Garry, where training and organisation proceeded throughout the winter.

In October Lt.Col. George French, Royal Artillery, late Commandant of the School of Gunnery at Kingston, was appointed Commissioner of the Force, and made his way west to join his command at Lower Fort Garry. It was his view that the most effective way to achieve control was to move the bulk of his command directly to the junction of the Bow and Belly Rivers, reportedly the location of 'Fort Whoop-Up', the base of the whiskey traders. It was also apparent that the size of the force must be increased if it was to succeed.

Authority was granted to recruit the Force up to its authorised strength of 300, and the remaining 150 men were recruited and assembled at Stanley Barracks, Toronto. A great many of the new men had seen previous military service and the three new divisions shaped up rapidly, except in equitation—which was a question of untrained men learning to ride untrained horses with too little time for either.

Permission was sought, and granted, to move the three new divisions by rail through the United States to the Manitoba border by way of Chicago,

Senior NCOs at Fort Walsh, 1878, wearing gold-laced 1876 pattern tunics and gold-banded dark blue pillbox caps, brown leather pouch belts and slings for 1853 pattern light cavalry sword. Seated centre, with Crimea medals, Sgt.Maj. J. Francis, who was reputed to have ridden in the Charge of the Light Brigade. (Glenbow Museum)

St. Paul and Fargo. They left Toronto on 6 June 1874 complete with horses and equipment, and arrived in Fargo on 12 June to begin the task of assembling wagons and harness, and loading stores. By the afternoon of the 14th the last division moved into camp some six miles from Fargo where the column assembled to march to Manitoba. On the evening of 19 June the Commissioner and his force arrived at Dufferin, Manitoba (now Emerson), where they were joined by 'A', 'B' and 'C' Divisions from Fort Garry. The entire Force was now together for the first time, and went into camp to prepare for the march west.

The next four weeks were busy ones for all ranks. Issues of clothing, arms and personal equipment were completed, and the divisions adjusted to equal strength. Prior to departure the entire Force, with the exception of the few men detailed to the Stone Fort (Lower Fort Garry) and Fort Ellice, was assembled for a full-dress ceremonial parade. This was the only occasion in the history of the Force when it paraded at full strength. Scattered in detachments over the West, and later over the whole nation, it was never again to parade united.

The March West

The preparations and ceremonies over, the Force readied itself for the long trek. The total strength stood at 318 all ranks. Detachments to Fort Ellice, Fort Garry, and the rear party at Dufferin left 275 officers and men for the march westward. With them went 114 Red River carts, 73 wagons, two 9-pdr. field guns, two brass mortars, and several reapers, mobile forges and kitchens. The beef ration was herded along on the hoof at the tail of the column.

Col. French's plan was to move as directly as possible to the forks of the Belly and Bow Rivers, to establish a post and leave a sufficient garrison to police the area, and to return to Fort Ellice with the balance of the Force to establish headquarters. Before leaving Dufferin Col. French received instructions to send part of his command to Edmonton, and Insp. Jarvis with 'A' Division was given this assignment. He was to leave the main column at Roche Percée and to proceed by way of

Fort Ellice and the general line of the North Saskatchewan River to Edmonton.

The Force headed west on 8 July, 1874. The heat of the summer and feeding on rough prairie grass, when it was to be found, soon began to take a toll on the horses and oxen: hardly a day passed without some beast dying on the trail. But the column moved steadily forward along the well-established

Jerry Potts, son of a Scots father and a Blood Indian mother, was born in c.1840; he served as a guide and interpreter for the NWMP from 1874, when he led the Force to 'Fort Whoop-Up', until his death in 1896. Engaged at Fort Benton by Asst.Comm. Macleod, he was invaluable in introducing the Force to the ways of the frontier. This photograph shows him in beaded buckskin, with his '76 Winchester. Potts was the first of many civilian members of the Force. (RCMP)

NWMP Band at Fort Battleford, 1884; in front, Sgt. Fred Bagley with 1853 pattern sword. Bagley, a keen amateur musician, was instrumental in forming a band which was a popular feature of local social gatherings apart from its martial duties. The musicians wear the full dress scarlet tunic and the dark brown fur winter cap with yellow hanging bag. (Glenbow Museum)

Supt. Samuel Benfield Steele, c.1890, in full dress. The son of a Royal Navy officer, Steele, a man of immense energy and stamina, was commissioned in the Canadian Militia in 1866 aged 15, but later served as a corporal during the Fenian Raids and Wolseley's 1870 expedition. He was promoted sergeant major NWMP in 1873, and inspector in 1878; raised Steele's Scouts during the 1885 rebellion; was promoted superintendent the following year; and commanded the NWMP in the Yukon during the 1898–99 gold rush. In the South African War he raised and commanded Lord Strathcona's Horse (made CB and MVO); and was a colonel in the South African Constabulary 1901–06, commanding Transvaal Division. He was a major-general, commanding 2nd Canadian Division, in 1915 (made KCMG) before his death in 1919. His autobiography Forty Years in Canada presents an engaging picture of a very formidable man who practised many of the best Victorian virtues in a highly pragmatic fashion. (Alberta Provincial Museum)

boundary trail, averaging about 26 miles a day. The daily routine was to move out early in the morning, sometimes at 3 a.m., to halt for several hours during the intense heat of midday to rest the animals, and then to march until early evening, halting at some spot where grass, water and wood were readily available. By the time the head of the column reached camp, carts, wagons, guns and cattle were strung out for miles. Each day Assistant Commissioner Macleod brought up the rear, shepherding the weakened horses and broken carts, sometimes reaching camp well after midnight.

In this fashion the column reached Roche Percée on 24 July having covered a distance of 270 miles. The Force camped on the banks of the Souris River and rested while 'A' Division left the main body and turned north for Edmonton.

On 31 July the column swung north of the Boundary Commission's main trail and headed into the unknown expanse of the prairies. The Metis guides were unfamiliar with the country beyond this point, so it was a matter of navigating with the aid of compass and Palliser's map of the West. After traversing a difficult stretch of country with little grass or water the column reached the Cypress Hills on 25 August, having covered 582 miles. They halted for several days in preparation for the last phase of the journey into the heart of the Blackfoot country.

On 1 September the column moved west in cold, wet weather. Buffalo were encountered in increasing numbers which solved the meat supply problem; however, the great beasts ruined all good pasture, and the horses and oxen weakened as the going became more difficult. The Force pressed on but by 10 September the horses were in poor condition and dying in increasing numbers. The Commissioner calculated that they had reached a position very close to the forks of the Bow and Belly Rivers, the location of the whiskey traders' Fort Whoop-Up. For the next two days scouting parties fanned out from the main body, but found no sign of traders or of the fort. If the column remained in the present inhospitable location for long, all of the horses would be lost; pasture had to be found quickly. The Commissioner decided to march to the Sweet Grass Hills, some 60 miles to the south-west. This destination was reached on 18 September, and the long march west was ended. The Force was 97 days out of Fargo and had travelled a distance of 1,009 miles.

Having reached a suitable site for winter quarters, it was decided to leave 'B', 'C' and 'F' Divisions under the command of Assistant Commissioner Macleod. The Commissioner would return east with 'D' and 'E' Divisions to establish headquarters.

With colder weather fast approaching, and a long trip ahead, the return party did not prolong their stay, but set out on the eastward journey on 21 September. The Commissioner and Assistant Commissioner Macleod went south to Fort Benton in the United States to pick up mail, horses and supplies for winter, and to communicate with Ottawa. After several days the Commissioner left Benton to rejoin the small column moving eastward, while Macleod remained to complete his business before returning to the main camp.

While in Fort Benton, Macleod learned the true location of Fort Whoop-Up: it lay at the forks of the Belly and St. Mary's Rivers some 70 miles to the west of its reported position. Macleod decided to move into the foothills at once to establish winter quarters. On 2 October he rejoined his slender force, bringing back from Benton, in addition to

horses and supplies, Jerry Potts, son of a Scottish father and an Indian mother, who became the guide and interpreter for the Force.

On 9 October Macleod's command reached Fort Whoop-Up, which was deserted except for the caretaker and an assistant: word of their coming had preceded the column, and the traders had left with their goods for winter quarters south of the boundary.

Macleod and his men moved out of Fort Whoop-Up in a north-westerly direction, and after travelling for three days came upon a broad loop of the Old Man's River which met all the requirements for a permanent camp. On this site, close to the present city of Lethbridge, Macleod constructed winter quarters, thus establishing Fort Macleod, and the permanent presence of the North-West Mounted Police in the Canadian West.

In the meantime, Commissioner French with his small column moved steadily eastwards, reaching Swan River, the proposed site of the headquarters of the Force, on 21 October. This location proved to be quite unsuitable for any sizeable number of men and animals. French left 'E' Division at Swan River, and returned to Dufferin via Winnipeg with the remaining men. This completed a round trip of 1,959 miles for the Commissioner and the men of 'D' Division.

Insp. Jarvis and the men of 'A' Division, who left

Full dress parade at the Depot, Regina, c.1888. Officers wear 1886 pattern uniforms with brown leather full dress waist and pouch belts. The band's helmet plumes are scarlet horsehair; later, in the 1890s, the band adopted a helmet plate. The bandsmen here wear a brown leather pouch belt, presumably supporting a music case. (RCMP)

the main body at Roche Percée on 24 July, toiled north and west along the reaches of the North Saskatchewan River. They encountered conditions equally formidable to those of the main column and, in a state of near collapse, arrived at the HBC Post at Fort Edmonton on 1 November after travelling almost 900 miles from Roche Percée. With the arrival of Jarvis in Edmonton, the Force was in a position to bring the North-West within reach of the law.

Further posts were set up, the major ones being Fort Walsh in 1875 and Fort Battleford in 1875–76, with others at Fort Calgary, Swan River, Fort Saskatchewan and Shoal Lake. Once they were established in the North-West the demands on the Force escalated; additional duties included the supervision of treaty payments, ensuring fair trading practices, providing limited relief and medical services to the Indians—much restricted by inadequate police-resources—as well as carrying out a network of patrols throughout the area.

The arrival of the NWMP had considerable economic and cultural impact on the small communities in the sparsely populated region of Western Canada. The most immediate effect was economic: the payroll and the purchase of supplies injected comparatively large amounts of money into the local economy wherever their posts were set up. Total expenditure for the Force was $335,000 in 1874–75. More importantly, the collective social and cultural values of the members of the Force became the dominant standards of the communities, and to a considerable extent influenced the style of development of Western Canada.

The members of the Force, recruited in Eastern Canada, in particular in Ontario, brought with them the mid-Victorian values typical of the society they left behind. These might be summed up as a belief in the superiority of British institutions such as law and order, parliamentary democracy and paternalistic imperialism. The latter had not yet been debased by jingoism and commercial necessities, and was favourably, if somewhat condescendingly, contrasted with the rough and ready 'Wild West' development of the Western United States, with its murderous Indian wars and municipal anarchy.

The officers as a group were predominantly men born in the United Kingdom and English-speaking Canadians from Ontario and Quebec, largely Church of England and well educated with some experience in the Militia. They were essentially from families with a military or professional background. NCOs and constables were nearly all British- or Ontario-born Protestants from commercial, industrial and agricultural backgrounds. They were young: the average age in 1877 was 25, and that of the officers was 31. Of the 55 officers commissioned between 1873 and 1880 only 19 were married during any portion of their service, an illustration of the contemporary prevalence of late marriage as well as the difficulties of combining family life with the career of an NWMP officer.

On leaving the Force many men settled in the West, thanks in part to the land grants given to those who completed their terms of service. These men in turn influenced the development of their communities. Thus, in addition to providing economic stimulus and establishing respect for the rule of law, the NWMP contributed what would today be called a 'WASP' set of values, which has been dominant to this day.

Mounted constable photographed at Regina, 1893, wearing yellow-banded blue pillbox, scarlet serge undress tunic, yellow-striped dark blue breeches, and black boots. The pistol lanyard is worn around the body. Details of the California stock saddle are clear, though the forward of the two cinches is largely hidden by the rider's leg. Wooden stirrups were worn very long. (Glenbow Museum)

The Task of the Mounted Police

The Indian peoples faced a period of harsh transition at this time. The buffalo, which was the staple of their existence and the *raison d'être* for their nomadic life, was fast disappearing and it was government policy to enforce a system of reserves on which it was hoped that the Indians would become peaceful farmers, thus making way for white settlement. This situation was complicated by the advance of settlement below the border and the Indian Wars in the United States. In 1876 the defeat of Col. George A. Custer at the Battle of the Little Bighorn by the Sioux and Cheyenne resulted in strong US Army counter-measures. The Sioux, under their leader Sitting Bull, retreated into Canada. This influx of a warlike nation, hostile to many of the Indian tribes on the Canadian side, and the risk of damage to relations with the United States led the NWMP into negotiations with the Sioux and the Americans. These culminated in face-to-face meetings at the NWMP post at Fort Walsh, which resulted in a peaceful solution, but hardly scratched the surface of the problem of the future of the Indians.[1]

The NWMP did what they could to relieve distress and starvation amongst the Indian people, and constantly reported their desperate plight to Ottawa—with, unfortunately, scant response.

The coming of the railway multiplied the tasks of the Force. Settlement increased: between 1881 and 1885 the white population expanded from 7,000 to 23,000. In addition the construction crews on the line had to be controlled and protected. Seventy men under Supt. Steele were sent to the junction of the Kootenay River and Wild Horse Creek, where they constructed the first NWMP post in British Columbia.

The North-West Rebellion, 1885
As early as July 1884 the NWMP were warning of Indian unrest due to the threat of starvation caused by the disappearance of the buffalo. Discontent was also reported among the *Metis* who had moved to Saskatchewan after the suppression of the Provisional Government in 1870. They again felt threatened by the spread of settlement, and feared that they would lose their lands under the newly proposed government survey. It was not the government's intention to dispossess the *Metis* or ignore their needs; but, as in 1870, consultation did not take place and local sensitivities were ignored.

The *Metis* were a unique people, of mixed Indian and French-Canadian blood, whose distinct culture left them separate from both their forebears. They were little understood in Eastern Canada and lacked a spokesman in Ottawa. On their invitation Louis Riel returned from exile to be their leader in what was hoped would be peaceful negotiations. However, their historical experience of the buffalo hunt had given them a commando-style organisation adaptable to guerrilla warfare.

The Mounted Police, who were spread out across the prairies in small detachments, were not organised or armed to suppress an uprising. The information they passed to Ottawa about local conditions and the concerns of the inhabitants of all races was ignored; and the rebellion broke out in March 1885, when the rebels seized the trading post at Duck Lake and demanded that Supt. Crozier at Fort Carleton surrender his post. Crozier's reaction was to march at once with 56 police and 43 men of the Prince Albert Volunteers to arrest the rebels. He walked into an unexpected ambush in which the

NWMP gun crews at drill, Fort Macleod, Alberta, 1894. This 9-pdr. RML was one of the two brought out on the 'March West' in 1874, and may have been the one fired in the engagement at Frenchman's Butte in 1885; its more usual rôle was firing ceremonial salutes. The brass mortar, right, was also part of the original armament of the Force in 1874. (RCMP)

Assistant Surgeon Charles Selby Haultain, *c*.1895, wearing the mess uniform of 1886 pattern: scarlet jacket with dark blue collar and cuffs, dark blue vest and trousers. Note NW Canada Medal 1885, and rank badges still worn on the collar at this date. (RCMP)

Sgt.Maj. Flintoff (left) and Supt. A. H. Griesbach at Fort Saskatchewan, *c*.1894. Flintoff wears the 1886 pattern NCOs' full dress, and the binocular pouch can be seen. The officer wears 1886 pattern full dress; note double Austrian knot at cuff, and plain leather sabretache slings. Griesbach, a veteran of the 15th Hussars and Cape Mounted Rifles, joined in 1873 and held Regimental Number 1; he allowed himself certain non-regulation flourishes, such as the black saddle fleece and the cavalry pattern saddle. (Alberta Provincial Museum)

Metis, under their able leader Gabriel Dumont, inflicted casualties of 12 dead and 11 wounded, forcing him to retreat.

Police detachments and local civilians were blockaded in the posts at Fort Battleford and Fort Pitt by Indians under their chief, Big Bear. Insp. Francis Dickens and his 25 men retreated from Pitt, leaving the civilians prisoner. Battleford was relieved by the arrival of a column of the North West Field Force, whilst another column defeated the rebels and captured Riel at Batoche on 9 May. Mounted Police detachments were in action at Cut Knife Hill, Batoche, Frenchman's Butte and during the pursuit of Big Bear. Supt. Sam Steele raised Steele's Scouts; former inspector John French raised French's Scouts, and was killed at Batoche.

In all the Force lost eight dead: at Duck Lake, Consts. T. J. Gibson, G. P. Arnold and G. K. Garrett; at Fort Pitt, Const. D. L. Cowan; at Cut Knife Hill, Cpls. R. B. Sleigh and W. H. T. Lowry and Const. P. Burke; at Fort Battleford Const. F. O. Elliott. Wounded at Duck Lake were Supt. L. N. F. Crozier, Insp. J. Howe, Cpl. T. H. Gilchrist, Consts. A. Millar, S. F. Gordon, J. J. Wood and A. Manners-Wood; at Fort Pitt, Const. C. Loasby; at Cut Knife Hill, Sgt. J. H. Ward. At Loon Lake, Sgt.

W. Fury; and at Frenchman's Butte, Const. D. McRae.

As a result of the rebellion any talk of disbanding the Force died away and the authorised strength rose to 1,000. The Depot Division was established on 1 November 1885 to train recruits at Regina, the headquarters of the Force since 1882. The budget was raised to $1 million, much of which went to erect new buildings in place of the old log buildings put up by the constables themselves at detachments throughout the West. Needless to say, the combined Headquarters/Depot Division received more than a fair share of new buildings—including the first riding school, completed in early 1886, where the Riding Master, Insp. W. G. Mathews, formerly 3rd Hussars, produced the first Musical Ride in 1887.

The position of Senior NCO of the Force was revived in 1886, to oversee the training programme, and was given to Sgt. Maj. Robert Belcher, who had joined in 1873 after service with the 9th Lancers. Belcher was in effect regimental sergeant major, and the predecessor of the present Corps Sergeant Major.

The Patrol System

In 1886 Lawrence William Herchmer was appointed Commissioner. Through the friendship of his family with the Prime Minister Sir John A. Macdonald, to which he owed his appointment, he obtained the political support needed to thoroughly re-organise the Force. This he accomplished, though at the cost of considerable internal friction. The patronage involved in appointments to the Force, and in the award of contracts for supplies, made it inevitable that political influence played a part in these matters: few applications for the Force were unaccompanied by recommendations from MPs, senators or other political figures. However, political interference in the conduct of actual police duties was minimal.

Herchmer, who had served in H.M. 46th Regiment for four years, and for eight years as an Indian Agent in Manitoba, was a disciplinarian with an abrasive personality, but an able administrator. Standing Regulations and Orders were published in 1889, recruiting standards were raised, training was greatly improved, and a pension plan for NCOs and constables introduced. His most important work was to adjust the services provided by the Force to meet the needs of crime prevention in the vast and sparsely populated area under his control. The military format was retained, but duties became almost entirely civil.

The patrol system was introduced so that the presence of the NWMP became familiar to every inhabitant, their co-operation being enlisted and every occurrence reported. This mass of paper was collated at Division headquarters to provide a detailed picture of what was happening in the region. This entailed continual horseback patrols, and in 1887–95 the Force covered as much as $1\frac{1}{2}$ million miles a year. The success of this system, and the consequent lack of crime, led to questions about the need for such a large police establishment and calls for economy. From 1,000 men in 1885 the Force was reduced to 750 by 1898, when the policing of the Yukon absorbed more than 250 of the total. This shortage of men coincided with a greatly increased influx of settlers, leaving the Force undermanned and far less effective than in the past.

In 1905 the provinces of Alberta and Saskatchewan came into existence. To accommodate the needs and jurisdictions of the new provinces the first contracts were negotiated for the Force to act under the direction of the provincial authorities to enforce the criminal law and local statutes.

The Yukon and the Klondike

The Yukon Territory has a common border with Alaska, which was purchased from the Russians by the United States in 1867. The presence of gold in the area had been fairly well known since at least 1886, when the first major strike occured. The

The NWMP contingent to the 1897 Jubilee, wearing the scarlet serge undress tunic (note high proportion of senior NCOs, indicated by gold-braided collars), armed with the '76 Winchester. The tight fit of tunic and breeches and the low cut of the boots were features of this uniform, worn with the Stetson for the actual parade. (Glenbow Museum)

NWMP post at the summit of the Chilkoot Pass on the route to Dawson city, Yukon Territory during the gold rush of 1898–99. The work was rough and hard, and the weather cold—as can be seen from the clothing worn here; smartness and formality came later, when permanent barracks were built at Dawson City. (Glenbow Museum)

NWMP sergeant, *c.*1900, probably at Whitehorse, Yukon Territory. He wears the dark blue pea-jacket over the scarlet serge undress tunic; fur cap, dark blue stockings and hide *mukluks* were part of official winter clothing issue. (Ernest Brown Coll., Yukon Archives)

Canadian Government was faced with the problem of establishing control, and hence sovereignty, in this remote region, fixing the so far ill-defined border with Alaska, and avoiding the type of social chaos which had occurred during the California gold rush.

The first contact of the NWMP with the Yukon was in 1894 when Insp. Charles Constantine was sent to investigate the situation. He reported that the tasks to be accomplished were the control of liquor and gambling, the collection of customs duties and the establishment of a police presence to enforce Canadian laws, preventing the development of an American frontier-style community, which the Canadian authorities feared would result in lawless anarchy.

Constantine returned in 1895 with 20 men to set up Fort Constantine, from which he exercised a benevolent despotism. This was firmly in place by the time of the Bonanza Creek find and the start of the Klondike Gold Rush in 1896. From the beginning the NWMP carried out nearly all the administrative functions of government, acting as customs collectors, land agents, magistrates, police, gaolers, and mail carriers, promulgating local ordinances regulating everything from Sabbath observance to gambling and prostitution, and issuing liquor licences.

The local headquarters of the Force was transferred in 1897 to Dawson City, which was the major centre of population adjacent to the gold fields. At the height of the gold rush Dawson had a population of 20,000 and in 1898 an estimated $6 million worth of gold was taken out. The miners were accompanied by all the people needed to provide services in this rich, bustling community. Storekeepers, outfitters, lawyers, hotelkeepers, construction workers and prostitutes flocked to Dawson. Hotels, stores, a theatre and a growing police barracks sprang up. This influx greatly increased the work of the NWMP, whose numbers grew to 285 by 1898; the desire of both merchants and miners for a stable, regulated society in which to carry on their business meant that the majority of the citizens supported the activities of the Force.

Supt. Sam Steele took over from Constantine in 1898, ruling the area with a paternal mixture of pragmatic common sense and Victorian morality. Liquor licences were restricted; gambling was regulated; law breakers, actual or potential, were set to work on the police wood pile, or abruptly told to get out of town; prostitution was tolerated, but confined to the red light district and medically supervised to a certain extent; and the carrying of guns was forbidden. The detachment at the Chilkoot Pass refused entry to the goldfields to any

The guardians of the Empire dressed for dinner in the Klondike as well as in the jungle: NWMP officers and prominent citizens of Dawson City pose in front of the officers' mess in the NWMP barracks, 1900. Rank badges are still worn on the collar of the scarlet mess jacket. All wear the Field Service cap in dark blue with a yellow top. (Public Archives of Canada Photo c.42775)

miner without a year's supply of provisions. The Sabbath was strictly observed: businesses shut down and all work stopped. As on the Prairies, the community accepted the NWMP rôle as police, judge and gaoler as a reasonable price for stable conditions, the more so since the Force met local wishes halfway and because the outlook and training of the officers prevented the development of any sort of police tyranny. By 1899, when the peak of the rush had passed, civil servants had arrived to relieve the Force of many administrative duties; and a militia unit, the Yukon Field Force, had arrived in May 1898, remaining until June 1900 to assist the police and to reinforce Canada's claim to sovereignty over the Territory.

(Dawson City eventually became almost a ghost town, but has revived in the last 20 years as a considerable tourist attraction, with many of the original buildings restored by Parks Canada.)

The South African War, 1899

In addition to many former members of the Force who served in the Boer War, 245 serving police-men saw service on leave of absence, mainly in the 2nd Canadian Mounted Rifles, commanded by Commissioner L. W. Herchmer and in Lord Strathcona's Horse raised and commanded by Supt. S. B. Steele, both with the rank of lieutenant-colonel. Four men were killed: Sgt. H. R. Skirving, Cpl. J. R. Taylor, Consts. Z. R. E. Lewis, and F Davidson; and three died of enteric fever, Cpl. G. M. O'Kelly, Consts. R. Lett and H. H. Clements.

The NWMP had a distinguished record in South Africa; honours included the Victoria Cross to Sgt. A. H. Richardson; the DSO to Supt. G. E. Sanders, Insp. A. C. Macdonell and Insp. F. L. Cartwright; the CB and MVO to Supt. S. B. Steele; the CMG to Insp. R. Belcher and Insp. A. M. Jarvis; the DCM to Sgt. G. Hynes, Sgt. Maj. Richards and Const. A. S. Waite.

The NWMP contributed to the build-up of the South African Constabulary during and after the war, four officers and 38 NCOs and constables served with the SAC, usually on leave of absence, including Supt. Sam Steele who was appointed to command the Transvaal Division with the rank of colonel.

The First World War

The government decided in 1914 that no leaves of absence would be granted to serving members of the Force, because of the need to maintain police services at home; but many former members served overseas in all arms of the services. In the spring of 1918 there was a need for cavalry re-inforcements and permission was given to release men for overseas. Twelve officers and 231 other ranks of the Force plus 495 new recruits were enlisted. In England the older members were formed into 'A' Squadron RNWMP and saw active service in France and Belgium, under the command of Supt. G. L. Jennings. The others went as reinforcement to existing units of the CEF, in particular the Fort Garry Horse, the Royal Canadian Dragoons and the newly formed Tank Corps.

In July 1918 'B' Sqn. RNWMP of six officers and 184 men was recruited to join the Allied Expeditionary Force intervening to support the White Russians in eastern Siberia. The squadron remained for a few months in Vladivostock without seeing any action, before being withdrawn in response to public pressure at home. Both squadrons wore RNWMP badges (see Plate F).

The Formation of the RCMP

In 1918 the government divided federal policing between the RNWMP and the Dominion Police, the latter being responsible for Eastern Canada and the RNWMP for the West and the Arctic. The strength of the RNWMP had been seriously depleted by the departure of 900 men to serve overseas in the Canadian Expeditionary Force, leaving only 300 men to cover all RNWMP duties.

The Dominion Police had its origins in the Western Frontier Constabulary, formed in 1864 at the height of the American Civil War to protect Canadian neutrality, which had been compromised by the Confederate raid on St. Albans, Vermont from across the border in Quebec. This body was mainly an intelligence-gathering agency, commanded by Gilbert McMicken. With the victory of the Union forces, the rôle of the Constabulary changed to monitoring the hostile activities of the Fenians—Irish Americans who hoped to obtain independence for Ireland by invading Canada, and so disrupting British-American relations that the British would grant major concessions. Plans were even made to hold part of Canada 'hostage' for this purpose. This agitation resulted in the Fenian raids of 1866 and 1870, and culminated in the assassination of D'Arcy McGee, a prominent Canadian politician. Success in combating Fenian activities was principally due to intelligence gathered by the Constabulary, which was transformed in 1868 into the Dominion Police Force, with McMicken as Commissioner. Between 1870 and 1914 the Dominion Police also became responsible for guarding government buildings and VIPs and, more importantly, for compiling criminal and fingerprint records.

Under Sir Arthur Percy Sherwood, Commissioner 1885–1919, security and intelligence duties during World War I grew into a major part of the work. At the same time the RNWMP was assigned

Insp. Scarth, Supt. Wood, Insps. Routledge and Starnes, and Assistant Surgeon Thompson at Dawson City in 1900. The officers wear the 1886 pattern dark blue undress tunic, as modified in 1896 with square-cut collar; the recently-approved brown Strathcona boots, and Stetsons. Thompson wears the scarlet Field Service Patrol Jacket. Note rank badges still worn on collar. (Public Archives of Canada Photo c.42765)

NWMP Surgeon, c.1902, in Khaki Field Service uniform, introduced as an alternative to the blue or scarlet frock, and identical to Militia issue. Buttons, rank badges and 'NWMP' shoulder titles were bronzed. Medical officers on the Headquarters Staff wore cherry gorget patches with a line of black braid, and a cherry band on the peaked forage cap. (RCMP)

security duties in the West, in particular the control of enemy aliens.

In 1918 economic and social pressures from labour and returning soldiers, coupled with the pervasive fear of Bolshevism, high unemployment and low wages, produced considerable unrest. This peaked in the Winnipeg General Strike of May 1919: one man was killed and 30 injured when the RNWMP attempted to break up a banned parade. This was a traumatic experience both for the Force—who saw their rôle as the prevention of violence—and for the government, which was horrified at civil bloodshed.

As a result it was decided that the whole question of safeguarding internal security should be overhauled. The RNWMP absorbed the Dominion Police Force, becoming the national police agency responsible for intelligence and security duties as well as normal police and crime prevention work. The strength of the Force was raised to 2,500 and

Staff Sgt. A. H. Richardson, VC (seated right) at Fort Battleford, Saskatchewan, 1905. He was awarded the VC for saving the life of a fellow member of Lord Strathcona's Horse at Wolve Spruit, South Africa on 5 July 1900. Background, the CO's House—see Plate D. The 7-pdr. bronze cannon was acquired by the Force in 1876, having originally accompanied Wolseley's Red River Expedition. (RCMP)

Headquarters was moved from Regina to Ottawa, leaving behind the Depot Division which was henceforth concerned entirely with training. This change of focus was marked by a new title, 'Royal Canadian Mounted Police'.

Training

From its inception in 1882 Depot Division had been primarily concerned with recruit training. In these early days recruits came mainly from the farms of Eastern Canada; they were used to hard manual labour, and capable of being quickly trained in horse management and care. Training was military in style with emphasis on strict obedience to orders and regimental loyalty. Over the years, as criminals became more sophisticated, so did the policemen. Though performance standards were continually raised, conditions of employment and work remained rigorous; physical hardihood was essential in the days before the automobile and air travel, and until the 1950s marriage was not permitted during the first five years of service.

Today the RCMP Academy trains many specialist personnel including Native Special Constables, as well as providing advanced training courses. Members are sent to outside institutions, in particular the universities, where, for example, law and commerce degrees equip them for commercial crime duties. Recruits are given a thorough introduction to the law, especially in the area of civil rights.

Intelligence and Security Operations

During the 1920s and 30s the chief target of intelligence activity was the Communist Party, at a time when the export of revolution by Soviet Russia was seen as a major threat. Nazi and fascist sympathisers were also kept under surveillance, and quickly rounded up on the outbreak of war in 1939. This work was carried out operationally by the criminal investigation branch; but the revelations of the Soviet defector Igor Gouxenko in 1945 of the nature and extent of Russian espionage highlighted the need for much greater attention to security. Between 1950 and 1956 many changes were made and the Directorate of Security and Intelligence came into being, reporting directly to the Commissioner.

The combination of police and intelligence duties

LEFT
RNWMP Const. B. J. O. Strong at Regina, 1910, in winter dress: fur cap and mitts, buffalo coat over brown drill fatigue tunic, sheepskin chaps over breeches, and felt-lined boots. (RCMP)

CENTRE
Supt. Gilbert Sanders at Fort Calgary, 1903. He wears the newly introduced peaked forage cap, dark blue with a yellow band; the black-braided dark blue undress tunic, and yellow-striped dark blue breeches. Probably the only member of the Force ever to wear a monocle, Sanders received the DSO for attempting to save the life of a fellow officer in South Africa. (Glenbow Museum)

RIGHT
Two RNWMP constables outside the guardroom at Fort Saskatchewan in 1904, wearing the yellow-piped dark blue Field Service cap without badge—note chinstrap. The bugler wears the brown cotton duck Field Jacket introduced in 1901, with brass buttons and silver collar badges; cut like a tunic, this was used for fatigues, stable duties and patrols, and if properly fitted could be smart as well as practical. (Alberta Provincial Museum)

has not always been a happy one. For the police, trained to uphold the law and prevent crime, operating at, or even beyond the edge of the law in the security field was difficult. Perhaps more importantly, accusations that legitimate democratic dissent was being confused with subversion by the police could undermine the reputation for impartiality on which the Force relied to secure the co-operation of the average citizen in carrying out its law enforcement and crime prevention duties.

Thus in several stages the Security Service was reorganised. In 1970 it was given a civilian chief, and in 1984 its functions were assumed by a new civilian agency—the Canadian Security Intelligence Service.

The Mounted Police and the Arctic

The Middle North and Arctic regions of the North American continent have been claimed by Canada at least since the early days of the Hudson's Bay Company, but the cost and difficulty of access meant that little was done to substantiate this claim until after 1900. Fortunately, the same conditions inhibited any other claimants. By 1890 the region had been penetrated by traders and whaling ships, and Arctic exploration activity by nationals of other countries intensified. The Mounted Police, with its experience in the Yukon and its long record of adaptability, was the natural agent for the government to use to establish control and Canadian sovereignty.

A patrol to York Factory on Hudson Bay was made in 1890, but a sustained thrust did not start until 1903, when a force under Supt. Constantine and Sgt. Fitzgerald established a post at Fort McPherson, near the mouth of the Mackenzie River. Fitzgerald visited the whaling settlement on Hershel Island in the same year. In the Eastern

Cpl. Bowler on patrol near the mouth of the Little Slave River, 1904. A certain informality prevailed on the trail, though apart from the slouch hat the corporal's clothing is all official issue: scarlet serge tunic, tan cord breeches, black boots and brown gauntlets. Note the wallets attached to the saddle horn, and the binocular case hanging from its rear. (BC Provincial Archives)

Arctic Supt. Moodie set up a post at Fullerton on the west coast of Hudson Bay. Gradually a patrol network was set up using dog teams. The advent of aeroplanes in the 1920s & 1930s greatly extended the scope and eased the burden of this work, but the use of dog teams was not finally discontinued until 1969.

The perils of Arctic travel were vividly emphasised by the tragic episode of the 'Lost Patrol' in 1910. Insp. Francis Fitzgerald, a very experienced officer (whose wife was an Inuit), with a guide, Sam Carter, and Consts. Kinney and Taylor, left Fort McPherson for Dawson, but died of starvation *en route*. Investigations revealed that the guide was inexperienced and lost his way, and that to increase speed Fitzgerald had lightened their sled loads by taking insufficient food. This tragedy was, however, the exception: thousands of miles were covered each year without mishap.

Today RCMP detachments are stationed throughout the Arctic, the most northern being at Grise Fjord on Ellesmere Island, nearly 700 miles inside the Arctic Circle.

The Second World War

In 1939, in accordance with previous arrangements, 155 RCMP marine service personnel volunteered to transfer to the Navy and Air Force, along with 33 ships and boats which were badly needed for coastal defence and air-sea rescue.

It was decided that the best way for the RCMP to contribute its expertise to the Army, without disrupting its police obligations at home, was through forming a provost unit for traffic control, police and security duties. From the many volunteers, 112 men were selected to fill the ranks of No. 1 Provost Company (RCMP) which sailed for England in December 1939 as part of the 1st Canadian Infantry Division. Faced with increasing responsibilities at home the RCMP was unable to provide reinforcements from its own ranks after 1942, and the gaps were filled through normal Provost Corps recruitment. This mixed unit saw active service in Italy, France and Germany. RCMP personnel wore RCMP badges and shoulder flashes on their battledress (see Plate F).

Part of the attrition of No. 1 Company was through promotion of 58 experienced RCMP members to staff positions in the Canadian Provost

Corps, to officer No. 2 Provost Company, 2nd Canadian Division, and to fill many of the grades of Provost Marshal throughout the Canadian Army. RCMP officers and other ranks retained the right to continue wearing RCMP badges and shoulder flashes in their new positions, whenever possible. Altogether 213 members of the Force served in the Canadian Provost Corps, of whom 12 died on active service and 13 were wounded.

Uniforms

The 'Norfolk jacket', 1873–76

Many of the traditions established in the early days of the NWMP were of military origin, in keeping with the quasi-military rôle of the Force, and with the previous service in the Canadian Militia and the British Army of many of its original members. These military traditions were nowhere more apparent than in the style of the uniforms of the Force, which closely followed the patterns of the British Army.

Any study of the early uniforms relies heavily on the evidence of actual uniforms surviving in museum collections, and on contemporary photographs. Fortunately the Mounted Police appear to have been avid customers both of itinerant photographers who visited their posts, and of the professional studios of William Notman in Montreal and W. J. Topley in Ottawa. Documentary material such as letters, diaries, orders, dress regulations and other written sources usually assume the contemporary reader's familiarity with

Const. Marshall outside the stable at Writing-on-Stone Post, 1912. This photograph shows the realities of life at a small RNWMP post on the prairies: rough log buildings, and a sturdy, shaggy-coated horse with frayed harness. The constable's clothing is much the same as a civilian's: Stetson, dark blue pea-jacket, leather chaps, and brown leather gauntlets. The saddle is a modified single-cinch California stock pattern. (RCMP)

Const. George Randolph Pearkes (later Maj.Gen., VC, CC, CB, DSO, MC), at Whitehorse, Yukon Territory in 1913. The brown fur cap with ear flaps and the dark blue stockings, often worn with moccasins, were standard winter wear. Note method of wearing pistol lanyard under both shoulder straps. One of the most distinguished alumni of the Force, which he left in 1914, Pearkes won his VC at Passchendaele in 1917 with the 5th Canadian Mounted Rifles. He was GOC 1st Canadian Division in 1940–42; Minister of National Defence in 1957–60; and Lieutenant Governor of British Columbia in 1960–68. (RCMP)

vital aspects, which are thus left unmentioned, to the subsequent confusion of today's readers. But documents do establish dates when patterns of uniforms were modified, and they do specify colours—an important supplement to black and white photographs, which, before the invention of panchromatic film in 1900, reproduced scarlet, dark blue and yellow in almost identical shades of grey.

In keeping with Sir John A. Macdonald's demand that the uniforms of the new police force be kept simple and practical, the Norfolk jacket was initially adopted as the tunic for all ranks. Similar to the well-known civilian jacket but buttoned to the neck and with a stand-up collar, it was issued to the

HRH Edward, Prince of Wales on a visit to Regina in 1919 with, right, Comm. Aylesworth Bowen Perry, CMG (1900–23). In 1920 the Prince became the first Honorary Commissioner of the RCMP. Perry joined the Force in 1882 as an inspector, serving in the 1885 Rebellion and in various commands; he presided with great skill over the transformation of the Force into a modern national police agency. Here he wears the dark blue Service Order uniform. Note 1896 cavalry sword carried by officer on left.

Canadian Militia in the 1860s. Contemporary photos support the complaints of its untidy and unsoldierly appearance, but for all that, it was a good choice for the uniform of the newly formed North West Mounted Police in 1873–4: made of heavy scarlet serge with a wool lining, it was warm, and had plenty of large pockets. The fact that it only fitted where it touched meant that it was at least comfortable. Issued from Militia stores with a dark blue collar (Plate A1), it was soon provided with brass 'NWMP' buttons. The cloth belt was usually replaced with a brown leather snake-clasp belt with 'MP' in raised letters. Dark blue cavalry pattern overalls with a double white seam stripe, or tan or grey cord breeches, black boots, and a pillbox cap or white helmet completed the uniform.

The contingent which joined the Force at Dufferin were clothed in the standard Canadian Militia infantry tunic, the 'chevron cuff' pattern first issued in 1870, or the frock. Wear and tear due to the rigours of the march west wore the uniforms to rags, and no authenticated examples of the original uniforms have survived—although a Norfolk jacket of later issue, belonging to Supt. L. N. F. Crozier is now preserved in the Bruce County Museum, Southampton, Ontario.

Considerable hardship must have been caused by the slowness of supplies of clothing. Mr John A. Martin, a former constable and a tailor in civilian life, recalled in an article in the 1933 issue of the *RCMP Quarterly* that hides were purchased from the Indians and that he made up suits of buckskin for everyone at Fort Mcleod in the fall of 1875.

Due to the lack of surviving records it is difficult to determine the exact details of clothing worn between 1874 and the arrival of new pattern uniforms in late 1876. It is probable that the Norfolk jacket, cord breeches and boots or moccasins were the principal items of dress. A listing of the items carried on the march in April 1876 is contained in a notebook of Sgt. Robert H. Giveen, now in the Glenbow Museum Archives. It is a copy of orders issued by Assistant Commissioner Macleod, as follows:

'Heavy marching order to be carried on saddle. In blanket rolled behind, 1 towel, piece of soap, comb, and 1 pr. overalls in rear wallet. 1 shoe, 30 rounds ball ammunition, oil rags and sponge in offside wallet, 1 shoe, 10 rounds ball ammunition,

urry comb and brushes, 1 pr. socks. Coat and cape
rolled over wallet. Nosebag and picket-rope on near
side, D hobbles on off. On man Norfolk Jacket,
breeches, boots and spurs, helmet; 20 rounds
ammunition in pouch. NCOs to wear glasses, men
to carry butchers knife in leg of boot (not on belt).

By order
James F. Macleod,
Asst. Commissioner.
April 1/76.

Cloaks rolled 40 in. ⎱ . . . Buckles on top
Capes ,, 34 in. ⎰
Blanket ,, 30 in. . . . Buckles on top points
to rear

In the Valise:

Near Side	*Off Side*
pair drawers	1 pair overalls
shirt	1 shirt
Plume case & plume	1 pair socks
pair socks	Two towels & soap
flannel vest	Two shoe brushes on top
pair gloves	of the roll.
Clothes brush	
Holdall complete	
Hair & brass brushes	
on top of the roll.	

In the Flap:

Near Side	*Off Side*
bolt spur	1 bolt spur
high low	1 high low
[ankle boot]	[ankle boot]
Tin of blacking	Button stick
Curry comb	Tin of paste
Horse rubber	Horse brush
Stable sponge	Pipe clay & sponge
Oil Can	Stable bag.

'Cloaks to be rolled in length 40 inches. Cape to
be folded separately length 34 inches, to be placed
on top of the cloak and buckled on by the outside
straps.'

Weapons and Saddlery

The original weapons were the .577 Snider-Enfield
carbine, Mk.III, and the .450 Adams revolver,
second model. The carbine was carried in a 'bucket'
on the right-hand side of the saddle. While this

Assist.Comm. G. L. Jennings, *c.*1938, in full dress uniform with
gold aiguillette of ADC to the Governor General. Note senior
officers' 'bullet-hole' braid on collar. The Wolseley helmet was
introduced for full dress after the First World War, replacing
the Universal Pattern white helmet, and was still in Dress
Regulations in 1942; however, an 'alternative full dress' with
the peaked cap and red serge tunic was also allowed, and
became the sole full dress after the Second World War.
Jennings served in South Africa, and commanded 'A' Sqn.
RNWMP in France and Belgium, 1918. (RCMP)

single-shot weapon was quite satisfactory for the
first few years, by 1878 many Indians were carrying
repeating rifles. To restore parity in firepower, the
Force experimented with Winchester rifles, and
finally adopted the .45-75 Winchester Model 1876
military carbine.

The first shipment of revolvers to reach the Force
at Dufferin was poorly packed and many weapons
were badly damaged. The armourers resorted to
cannibalism to produce enough serviceable weapons for the march west, and the shortage was made
up by local purchase at Fort Benton. Maj.Gen.
Selby Smith, in his report to the Minister of Justice
in 1875, noted that recruits had been provided with
the improved Smith and Wesson revolver; however,
there had been problems with the weapon, and it

Commissioner from 1938 to 1951, Z. T. Wood, CMG, wears dark blue Service Order uniform; note double row of embroidered maple leaves on cap peak, and rank insignia of Commissioner on shoulder strap. Wood, too, had served with 'A' Sqn. in France. (RCMP)

was the General's view that the improved Adams should be issued to all ranks. The precise pattern of the Smith and Wesson was not mentioned, but authorities on the subject think it may have been the .44 calibre Smith and Wesson American Model. A shipment of the .450 calibre Adams revolver, third model, was received in 1875, and the Force was completely equipped with this weapon.

On several occasions during the early years some troopers found themselves armed with the lance, a most unlikely weapon for police work on the prairies. On the march west 20 picked men were formed into a corps of lancers to impress the Indians as the column moved into the Blackfoot country. A photograph of 1878 shows a troop on parade with lances at Fort Walsh, with the red-over-white swallow-tail pennon still in use today by the RCMP Musical Ride; but the lance soon became relegated to ceremonial parades and gymkhana events. The

original lances had bamboo shafts, and were probably tipped with the 1868 pattern point, still used today.

Officers carried the 1822 pattern British light cavalry sword with a steel hilt and scabbard, the blade decorated with 'NWMP', a buffalo head and the motto 'Maintiens le droit'. These were supplied by the London firm of Maynard, Harris & Grice. NCOs also wore swords, the 1853 other ranks' cavalry pattern with steel hilt and scabbard. Swords were not a regular issue to constables, though there appear to have been sufficient in store for sword drill to have been performed in training.

A small artillery detachment was formed to operate the two 9-pdr. RML guns and the two brass mortars brought out on the march west. The 9-pdrs. were considered by some to be of doubtful utility: Insp. Denney wrote that they '. . . gave us more trouble and crippled more horses than all the rest of the transport'. Commissioner French had counted on using them to storm Fort Whoop-Up if resistance was offered by the whiskey traders.

The Force left Dufferin equipped with the British Army Universal saddle; however, it had some marked deficiencies. The steel stirrups and buckles rusted easily, and were unbearably cold and slippery with ice in winter. It was not suited for rough work, and rolled from side to side. The Commissioner preferred the 'McClellan' saddle of the US Army and several were purchased for user trials, but not adopted. A number of California saddles with Texas rigging were obtained at Benton, and proved so satisfactory with their comfortable seat and double cinch (girth) that this saddle was adopted by the Force. With the introduction of the California saddle the carrying of the carbine moved from the 'bucket' to a strap fastened to the pommel.

New uniforms, 1876

During 1875 the need for appropriate uniforms to replace the hastily acquired garments of 1873 became pressing. The lack of differentiation between officers and men led to cases of insubordination being explained by constables on the grounds that they could not identify officers. The officers also wanted a distinctive and impressive uniform in keeping with their social, a

1: Constable, 1874
2: Inspector, full dress, 1876 ptn.
3: Inspector, undress, 1876 ptn.

A

1: Staff Sgt., undress, 1876 ptn.
2: Constable, full dress, 1879
3: Constable, 'scarlet serge', 1878

B

1: Staff Sgt., full dress, 1886
2: Superintendent, undress, 1890
3: Sgt.Maj., undress, 1890

C

1: Superintendent, full dress, 1886
2: Inspector, full dress, 1910
3: Constable, patrol dress, 1890

D

1: Constable, Golden Jubilee, 1897
2: Constable, full dress, 1910
3: Veterinary Surgeon, Service Order, 1904

E

1: Asst. Commissioner, full dress, 1930
2: Trooper, B Sqn. RNWMP; Siberia, 1919
3: Sgt., No.1 Provost Co.; UK, 1942

F

1: Superintendent, full dress, 1967
2: Superintendent, Review Order, 1967
3: Superintendent, mess kit, 1967

3

1

2

G

1: Constable, Service Order, 1960
2: Female constable, full dress, 1987
3: Constable, full dress, 1987

3

1

2

well as their military status; and a smart uniform for other ranks would be an aid in recruiting and re-enlistment. In the field, adequate protection against the extreme cold of the prairie winter was obviously essential.

At that time it was customary in Canada for Militia units to have a large say in the choice of their uniforms, and the Mounted Police followed this practice. The officers chose a very elaborate full dress (see Plate A2), the tunic being of British hussar pattern in scarlet with gold frogging and braid, dark blue trousers, a gold lace pouch belt and a beautifully embroidered pouch, the whole topped with a white India-pattern cork foreign service helmet with a white horsehair plume. A costly scarlet and gold sword belt and slings supported the 1822 pattern sword in a steel scabbard. A smart everyday undress uniform (see Plate A3) was also authorised. Scarlet was chosen for the tunics of all ranks, partly because it was the traditional British military colour, partly to avoid confusion with the blue-clad US Army during any dealings with the Indians. Stars and crowns on the collar, combined with varying patterns of sleeve and collar braid, indicated officers' ranks.

Ordered from Messrs. Maynard, Harris & Grice of 126 Leadenhall St., London during 1876, the uniforms arrived in early 1877. The invoice for Supt. James Walsh's complete set, including mess kit, totalled £105 17s. 9d. Despite a number of complaints about the quality of workmanship, this company continued to supply uniforms for all ranks for a number of years. Surviving examples of both full dress and undress tunics are made of materials of fine quality; and the lack of wear seems to indicate that full dress was worn comparatively seldom. The aim of differentiating between officers and other ranks was achieved: sergeants and above wore a scarlet infantry full dress tunic of good quality wool fabric, with gold lace and braid on collar and cuffs (see Plate B1); or an undress tunic of scarlet wool serge with gold collar lace only. A brown leather pouch belt with black binocular case, and an 1853 pattern cavalry other ranks' sword completed their distinctions. The full dress for constables and corporals (see Plate B2) included a scarlet tunic of good quality wool fabric with yellow collar and cuff braid, and the white 'Indian' or 'Ashantee' pattern foreign service helmet, worn without a badge.

The *St. Roch* was built as an RCMP Arctic supply ship in 1928. Under the command of Sgt. H. A. Larsen she sailed in 1940 from Vancouver, arriving in Halifax in late 1942 via the North West Passage—the first vessel to do so from west to east. Again under Larsen's command, she made the return journey of 7,295 miles in 86 days in 1944. She is preserved at the Vancouver Maritime Museum, in the care of Parks Canada. Insp. (later Supt.) Henry Absjorn Larsen, skipper of the *St. Roch* in 1940–44, is shown here in full dress uniform. Among his medals are the Atlantic and Pacific Stars, and the octagonal Polar Medal with bars 'Arctic 1940–42' and 'Arctic 1944'. (RCMP)

Uniform changes, 1882

In 1882 the Force adopted in place of the Adams the .476 Enfield Mark II revolver, a superior weapon which remained standard until 1905. There was a slight modification to the constable's full dress tunic, its yellow shoulder cords being replaced by a yellow-braided scarlet cloth strap; this tunic remained in use, otherwise unchanged, until 1904. The major change was to the uniform of senior NCOs: the 1876 full dress tunic was abandoned in favour of one of identical cut to that of the constables, but with gold-braided collar and cuffs; and an 1822 pattern cavalry sword in a black leather scabbard with steel mounts replaced the 1853 pattern (see Plate C1 for this uniform).

Officers' uniforms, 1886

Dress Regulations of 1886 authorised a less costly set of uniforms. The hussar-style full dress was replaced by a dragoon-pattern uniform (see Plate D1) with scarlet collar and cuffs, worn with a brown leather pouch belt and black binocular case; and brown leather sword belt and slings, also worn with undress. Rank badges were altered as follows: *Commissioner* crown and star on collar, triple Austrian knot on cuff; *Assistant Commissioner* crown, triple knot; *Superintendent* two stars, double knot; *Inspector* star, single knot. (The NWMP retained collar rank badges although the Canadian Militia had already followed the British Army in moving them to the shoulder straps.)

Although the pillbox cap was retained, a folding Field Service cap was introduced for undress, in dark blue with a yellow top. A dark blue universal cavalry pattern undress tunic, with black braid, was also authorised (see Plate C2); and a more practical single-breasted scarlet serge Patrol Jacket for Field Service was adopted as working uniform. Brown leather gauntlets replaced white. Medical officers were ordered to wear black waist and pouch belts with a black instrument case.

Officers' uniforms, 1890

The next Dress Regulations seem to represent the

LEFT
RCMP constable in winter clothing, 1960; brown fur cap, dark blue nylon parka with down-filled quilted lining, wool trousers and hide *mukluks*. The parka replaced the old buffalo coat for cold weather use, except for some ceremonial duties. (RCMP)

CENTRE
Winter uniform, 1960, with the buffalo coat worn since the 1870s; though warm, they were heavy, and by 1960 buffalo hides were scarce. From this date they were kept for parades and duties where the need for smartness ruled out the parka. Note brown Strathcona boots, yellow-striped blue breeches and brown fur cap. (RCMP)

RIGHT
Drum Major (Const.) C. Schrumm in Review Order, 1960. The purple shoulder belt is laced and embroidered in gold with the Division name 'Ottawa', and the battle honours 'North West Canada 1885', 'South Africa 1899–1902', 'France & Flanders 1918', and 'Siberia 1919'—but 'Europe 1939–45' is strangely missing. The badge on the right sleeve indicates a drum major, in the RCMP an appointment or qualification rather than a rank. (RCMP)

defeat of a move towards simpler and less costly uniforms. Brown leather waist and pouch belts were now relegated to undress only; for full dress, gold laced belts with purple centre lights and matching slings were authorised, and the embroidered full dress pouch was reintroduced. A helmet plate appeared, of the same design as the undress pouch badge.

A white twill summer Patrol Jacket for Field Service was authorised alongside the scarlet pattern; and officers were also permitted to wear khaki patrol jackets and breeches for patrol duty. The use of black Persian lamb gauntlets, and caps of the same fleece with a yellow 'bag', as introduced for winter wear in 1886, was continued.

The distinctions of medical officers were changed to black leather waist belts with two lines of gold lace, and matching slings; and a black pouch belt with three gold lines for Senior Surgeons, two for Assistant Surgeons. Veterinary Surgeons were to wear white patent leather waist and pouch belts and slings, and black leather instrument cases.

Rank badges were unchanged, though Senior Surgeons are now listed as wearing two stars, Assistant and Veterinary Surgeons one—presumably in acknowledgement of existing practice.

1904 Dress Regulations

Because the nature of their work subjected the clothing of the NWMP to unusually hard wear, there was continual correspondence between field detachments and Headquarters on the subject of suggested improvements. In the period 1899–1904 experience in the Klondike and South Africa helped to bring about major changes. In 1900 the following changes in other ranks' uniforms were listed in the Commissioner's Annual Report:

Discarded:
White helmet; pillbox cap; white gauntlets and gloves; full dress scarlet tunic; black riding boots; greatcoat; black fur cap; moccasins.

Adopted:
Stetson felt hat; Field Service cap; brown leather gauntlets and gloves; four-pocket serge frock tunic; brown Strathcona boots; pea-jacket; fur cap (Klondike pattern with earflaps); brown duck four-pocket Field Service tunic and cord breeches; elk

Two constables in Winter Review Order raising the then-new Canadian maple leaf flag, February 1965. They wear the scarlet serge tunic, brown fur hat, yellow-striped blue breeches, and 'stripped' Sam Browne equipment—i.e. without revolver. (RCMP)

mitts with wool mitts inside; slicker (raincoat) and sou'wester.

These changes were mainly the confirmation of actual practice in the field; e.g. the Stetson and Strathcona boots had been worn in the Klondike since 1898. Tunic collars were now higher, square-cut and fastened by two hooks and eyes. Breeches changed from the old form-fitting type, flaring out above the knee in the now-standard cut of riding breeches. Equipment was also up-dated: in 1895 the Force purchased 200 Lee-Metford .303 magazine carbines as a possible replacement for the Winchester. The NWMP inherited some Lee-Enfield .303 Mark I magazine rifles from the Yukon Field Force in 1900, and more were purchased; by 1904 this had become the standard arm of the Force. The leather cavalry pattern bandolier, with some loops for revolver ammunition, was worn over the left shoulder. In 1905 the Colt New Service .45

Staff Sgt. R. R. Cave in Mounted Service Order, 1970: dark blue tunic, brown officer's pattern Sam Browne and gauntlets, yellow-striped dark blue breeches, brown Strathcona boots. In full dress or 'Review Order' the scarlet tunic would replace the dark blue. The Colonial pattern saddle has a dark blue cloth with yellow edging and conjoined 'MP'; the 1908 pattern cavalry sword is attached to the saddle in a brown leather scabbard.

calibre revolver replaced the Enfield, and Sam Browne equipment was issued to carry it.

NCOs' uniforms changed in the same fashion as constables' and all wore a smaller version of the cap badge as collar badges, in blackened silver on the brown duck tunic, in brass on all others. Sergeant Majors were now permitted to wear a dark blue four-pocket frock tunic on certain duties, their chevrons on a red ground. Worsted chevrons were worn on the brown tunic.

Officers' uniforms were modified along the same lines. Full dress remained the same as under 1890 Dress Regulations, retaining the white helmet, but all ranks now wore a single Austrian knot on the sleeve. Force collar badges replaced rank badges, which were moved to the gold plaited shoulder cords (Plate D2). This uniform was kept for ceremonial duties; when parading with other ranks in the new full dress officers wore Review Order—the Stetson, scarlet frock, Strathcona boots, etc.

A dark blue frock tunic (Plate E3) similar to the

scarlet serge replaced the dark blue universal cavalry pattern undress tunic; and a peaked forage cap, dark blue with yellow band (cherry for medical officers, maroon for veterinary surgeons at Headquarters) and gold embroidered badge replaced the pillbox. The term 'scarlet serge' had by now come into use to describe the tunics worn by all ranks, whether of serge or other wool fabric.

During this period the 1896 officers' pattern British Army cavalry sword came into use with a steel scabbard for full dress, and with a brown leather-covered scabbard when worn with the Sam Browne.

The Royal North-West Mounted Police

In 1904 the NWMP was granted the designation 'Royal' in recognition of its members' services in the South African War; this entailed the addition of 'Royal' to the title on all badges and buttons, and brass shoulder titles changed from 'NWMP' to 'RNWMP'. The major change was to the facing colour on all tunics. The whole collar, the shoulder straps and the cuffs on officers' tunics changed to dark blue. On other ranks' tunics the shoulder straps became dark blue but the collar remained scarlet with dark blue gorget patches, a measure designed to cut the costs of conversion and to differentiate officers from other ranks.

Uniforms of the RCMP

With the change of title in 1920, 'Royal Canadian Mounted Police' appeared on buttons and badges, and shoulder titles changed from 'RNWMP' to 'RCMP'. Although everyday working uniforms became steadily more practical in the inter-war period, officers' full dress, though optional, was retained and even elaborated for senior ranks, such items as a cocked hat and frock coat being introduced. Wearing of full dress (Plate F1) was restricted to special parades and such ceremonial duties as accompanying the Governor General as an ADC on his more formal appearances.

The 1908 British Army cavalry pattern sword was carried by officers and senior NCOs, and the Wolseley helmet replaced the old 'Ashantee' pattern. Officers made increasing use of the undress dark blue tunic, now cut like the standard Army khaki service dress tunic with an open collar, worn with a white shirt and dark blue tie. The brown

Service Order tunic, similarly cut, became the daily working uniform, worn with either the peaked cap or the Stetson.

The use of the scarlet serge by constables was gradually limited to full dress occasions and the brown tunic was worn for most duties, with a light tan shirt and dark blue tie. This remains the principal uniform today (Plate H1).

The problem of cold weather clothing was met by increasing the numbers of layers of undergarments, usually wool, under the buffalo coat. The men were not relieved of carrying around this considerable weight until the appearance of down-insulated nylon parkas in the late 1950s. In the Arctic, clothing based on the garments worn by the Inuit and Indians, which utilised the principle of air entrapment to retain body warmth, was widely used. The 1928 Dress Regulations list the following standard issue:

Sweaters or windbreakers	1
Tuques (knitted wool caps)	1
Shirts, Makinaw	2
Kouletahs (under-parka of hide with fur inwards)	1
Artikis (outer parka, fur outwards)	1
Pants, heavy, deer skin	1
Pants, light, deer skin	1
Mitts, heavy, deer skin	2
Mitts, light, deer skin	2
Socks, light, deer skin	2 pr
Socks, heavy, deer skin	2 pr

Short and long duffle socks were an alternative issue for the deer skin items. The hide clothing was made up by native people and purchased locally. The drawback was that this type of clothing needed continual repair, the task of a man's wife in the Inuit family. RCMP patrols sometimes included wives of Inuit guides for this purpose.

Full dress for officers was still included in the 1942 Dress Regulations but after the Second World War it was dropped, and the uniforms shown in Plates G & H became the standard still worn today. The major innovation was the Review Order uniform for female members (Plate H2); for all other orders of dress women wore similar clothing to males. In 1970, to reflect the bilingual nature of Canadian society, 'Gendarmerie Royale du Canada' appeared on shoulder flashes, and metal shoulder titles were altered to 'GRC-RCMP'.

Insignia

Officers' rank badges since 1903

From the beginning the Force had used the same crowns and stars as the Militia, who in turn followed exactly the practice of the British Army. The military background and experience of many officers of the Force inclined them to value army rank above their Mounted Police rank: in official correspondence Commissioner Macleod was usually referred to as 'Col. Macleod', his former Militia rank. As late as 1923, when Commissioner Perry retired he was promoted major-general and was known in retirement as 'Gen. Perry.'

The effect of these military traditions was a desire on the part of the officers of the Force to have a clearly visible parity with military officers, in the shape of rank badges. As the Force expanded the Commissioner rose from wearing the same rank insignia as an Army colonel in 1876 to that of a lieutenant-general in 1987.

In 1903 the system of acknowledging seniority in a rank was introduced by a 'step up' in insignia, thus avoiding the costly need to create new ranks. This system apparently became confusing, with as many as three different ranks being indicated by identical insignia; eventually new ranks were introduced and the system was simplified.

In 1903 badges were revised in order to retain equivalency with the Militia, whose highest rank was now major-general, and to recognise seniority. Insignia were moved from the collar to the shoulder straps, in gilt metal except for full dress, when silver

(Left) First button, brass, used on Norfolk jacket from 1874. (Right) NWMP button incorporating buffalo head, as suggested by Comm. Macleod, probably introduced with 1876 pattern uniforms. With the accession of King Edward VII the crown became the King's type; after 1904 'RNWMP' replaced 'NWMP'; the King's crown was worn from 1920 to 1952; and the 'EIIR' button in use since 1954 features the RCMP crest.

embroidered stars and crowns were combined with a single Austrian knot on the cuff for all ranks:

Commissioner	Crown, two stars
Assistant Commissioner	Crown, star
Superintendent	Crown
Inspector	Star
" (with 10 years in rank)	Two stars
Surgeon	Crown
Assistant Surgeon	Star
" (10 years in rank)	Two stars
Veterinary Surgeon	One Star
" (10 years in rank)	Two stars

In an effort to avoid creating new ranks further changes were made in 1909:

Inspectors; Assistant & Veterinary Surgeons:

With 5 years in rank	Two stars
With 10 years in rank	Three stars

In the 1920s additional recognition was accorded to long service by means of insignia which raised the status of Mounted Police officers in relation to their military counterparts, by no means a negligible social consideration in those days. (This may have been a substitute for significant pay increases.) The Regulations of 1928 show:

Commissioner	Crown, two stars
Assistant Commissioner	Crown, star
Superintendent	Crown
" (5 years in rank)	Crown, star

1876 pattern tunic sleeve and collar braid, in gold lace. (Left) Commissioner—with crown on collar; Assistant Commissioner—with star. (Centre) Superintendent—with crown on collar. (Right) Inspector—with star on collar.

Inspector	Two stars
" (5 years in rank)	Three stars
" (15 years in rank)	Crown
Surgeon	Three stars
" (10 years in rank)	Crown
" (20 years in rank)	Crown, star
Assistant Surgeon	Two stars
Veterinary Surgeon	Two stars
" (5 years in rank)	Three stars
" (15 years in rank)	Crown
Assistant Veterinary Surgeon	Two stars

Commissioner Sir James MacBrien (1931–38) introduced the new ranks of Deputy Commissioner and Sub-Inspector in order to simplify some of this overlapping system of insignia, and to ease the way for promotion by merit as well as by seniority. Veterinary surgeons had apparently given way to civilian vets as horses gave way to automobiles. The 1942 Regulations show:

Commissioner	Crown, three stars
Deputy Commissioner	Crown, two stars
Assistant Commissioner	Crown, star
Superintendent	Crown
" (5 years in rank)	Crown, star
Inspector	Three stars
" (15 years in rank)	Crown
Sub-Inspector	One star
Surgeon	Crown
Assistant Surgeon	Two stars
" (5 years in rank)	Three stars

Ranks and insignia remained unchanged until 1960, when the new rank of Chief Superintendent

Pouches worn by officers and senior NCOs. (1) NWMP officers' full dress pouch, 1876 pattern: purple velvet flap, gold lace and embroidery, silver buffalo head. (2) RNWMP officers' pouch, the same as above but slightly larger and with added 'Royal'. After 1920 the inscription became 'Royal Canadian Mounted Police', but since the pouch became an optional item examples are very scarce. (3) 1876 pattern black binocular pouch, worn by officers with undress. (4) Senior NCOs' brass pouch badge worn with full and undress uniforms on pouch similar to but slightly longer than officers'. (RCMP)

was created between Superintendent and Assistant Commissioner. Inspectors and Sub-Inspectors were given more senior insignia, allowing the introduction of military general officers' insignia for the Commissioner and Deputy Commissioner, thus:

Commissioner	Crown, sword and baton
Deputy Commissioner	Star, sword and baton
Assistant Commissioner	Crown, three stars
Chief Superintendent	Crown, two stars
Superintendent	Crown, star
Inspector	Crown
Sub-Inspector	Three stars

This system of insignia remains in use today.

A distinction enjoyed by the Mounted Police is to provide aides-de-camp to the Governor General of Canada and to the Lieutenant Governors of the Provinces, all of whom represent the Sovereign in their jurisdictions. A gold aiguillette is worn on the right shoulder in full dress with the scarlet tunic, and with the dark blue tunic in Service Order.

NCOs' rank badges since 1876

NCOs' rank badges have changed little over the years. Chevrons and crowns are still used to denote non-commissioned ranks in a system similar, though not identical to that of the Victorian British Army. In 1876 non-commissioned ranks were:

Sergeant Major	Four-bar chevron below crown, point down, above cuff
Senior Staff Sergeant	Four-bar chevron below

	crown, point up, above cuff
Staff Sergeant	Four-bar chevron, point up, above cuff
Sergeant	Three-bar chevron below crown, point down, above elbow
Corporal	Two-bar chevron, point down, above elbow

These ranks existed from 1873 to 1875, and these badges were probably used during this period as well. Until 1882 badges were worn on both sleeves, though some photographs show them occasionally worn on the right sleeve only. After 1882 they were worn on the right sleeve only in all cases. Chevrons were of gold lace and crowns of gold embroidery, worn on a dark blue background on the scarlet tunic. On the greatcoat insignia were of yellow worsted, and sergeants' and corporals' badges were worn on the cuff so as to be visible below the deep cape. Badges of appointment and qualification were worn superimposed on the chevrons, except in the case of corporals, who wore them above the rank badges.

Ranks and insignia remained unchanged until 1903, with the exception of the reintroduction in 1882 of the rank of Regimental Sergeant Major, Senior Staff Sergeant then becoming Division Sergeant Major.

In 1903 the Regimental Sergeant Major wore a crown only, on the right forearm, and Division Sergeant Majors wore a four-bar chevron below a crown, point down, above the cuff. Other rank insignia were unchanged. Chevrons were gold on dark blue for scarlet tunics, gold on scarlet for dark blue tunics and pea-jackets, and yellow worsted on the brown field jacket.

In the 1920s brass one-third-size NCO rank badges were introduced for wear on the fur coat and slicker. Badges of appointment moved to a position just above the chevrons and below the crown, instead of being superimposed on chevrons. Chevrons continued to be worn on the right only, the left sleeve being reserved for five-point service stars above the elbow, and marksmanship badges above the cuff.

In 1960 the Corps Sergeant Major followed the practice of Army RSMs and adopted the insignia of the Royal Arms of Canada on the forearm; Staff

Sergeant Majors now wore a wreathed crown in the same position. Rank badges today are as follows:

Corps Sergeant Major	Royal Arms, above cuff
Sergeant Major	Four-bar chevron below crown, point down, above cuff
Staff Sergeant Major	Wreathed crown, above cuff
Staff Sergeant	Four-bar chevron, point up, above cuff
Sergeant	Three-bar chevron below crown, point down, above elbow
Corporal	Two-bar chevron, point down, above elbow

Badges of appointment

Worn by constables on the upper right arm, these proliferated over the years; in 1979 the Dress Regulations still showed Farrier and Saddler badges, as well as the following list of others, but by 1982 only those shown thus (*) survived:

Farrier/Veterinary	Horseshoe
Saddler	Horse bit
Rough Rider*	Spur
Drill Instructor	Crossed swords
Bandsman*	Lyre
Instructor (academic)*	Wreathed Gothic 'I'
First Aid Instructor	Wreathed Maltese cross
Musical Ride*	Crossed lances
Drum Major*	Lyre on crossed staff and sash over drum
Swimming Instructor	Wreathed crossed paddle and grappling hook on lifebelt
Air Division	Winged Pegasus on shield
Dog Master*	Dog's head in circle
Trumpeter	Crossed trumpets
Driving Instructor	Wreathed wheel
Physical Training Instructor	As for Drill Instructor

All are in gold on dark blue for the scarlet tunic; gold on scarlet for the dark blue tunic (senior NCOs); and yellow worsted on dark blue for the brown tunic.

An eight-point star was formerly the badge of a

quartermaster. The red Geneva cross on a white disc was worn by hospital stewards and attendants before 1940, when civilian staff of the Department of Veterans' Affairs began to take over the Force's medical needs.

Two badges are today worn on the left breast above the pocket and any medal ribbons. The Marine Division badge is a crown above 'Marine', a wreathed anchor to the left and a ship's wheel to the right. The Air Pilot's badge, embroidered in yellow silk on dark blue for all colours of tunic, had 'RCMP' within an oval maple wreath between wings; in 1976 gold replaced yellow embroidery, the lettering changed to 'RCMP-GRC', and a crown was added above the wreath.

NWMP constable's scarlet tunic with yellow braid, 1882 pattern; this is the same as the 1876 pattern except that the shoulder straps are now scarlet cloth edged with yellow braid. No collar badges or shoulder titles were worn. The waist belt was brown leather with a steel buckle; the white cross strap supports the haversack. In use until 1901, this was the 'scarlet coat' so familiar across the Canadian Prairies. (Glenbow Museum)

The Plates

A1: Constable, 1874
Based on a contemporary photograph of Const. Archibald Hare wearing the first 'Norfolk jacket' uniform; the blue collar (here shown turned down) is copied from the only known surviving example, that of Supt. Crozier, and is less than obvious in early photographs taken without panchromatic film. Breeches might be tan, grey, white or dark blue, all these colours being issued. The cloth belt was usually replaced by a brown leather belt to support the holster when on duty.

A2: Inspector, officer's full dress, 1876 pattern
Based on a photograph of the famous Sam Steele. There was no full dress sabretache; the undress pattern was worn from plain brown undress slings when mounted. Note light brown band around helmet.

A3: Inspector, officer's undress, 1876 pattern
The everyday working uniform; the tunic fastened with a series of hooks and eyes. The black patent leather binocular case was worn on the pouch belt, with a gilt badge. Based on a photograph of Insp. E. D. Clarke.
Background: Lower Fort Garry, the Hudson's Bay Company headquarters at Red River where the first contingent of the NWMP trained in 1873–74— the birthplace of the Force, preserved today as a national historic site by Parks Canada.

B1: Staff sergeant, undress, 1876 pattern
When worn with the pillbox cap, the 1876 full dress tunic constituted a version of undress; for full dress it was worn with the white helmet, brown leather waist belt and holster. Chevrons, officially worn on the right sleeve only, are seen in some photographs on both sleeves; note apparently white backing here. The 1853 pattern British cavalry sword in a steel scabbard was for ceremonial rather than for use.

B2: Constable, full dress, 1879
The full dress uniform introduced in 1876 remained little changed until 1903. The white linen haversack, often worn rolled up on parade, was a

distinctive feature of full dress as well as a practical carry-all on other occasions. The tunic was of good quality wool, and was chosen for its smart appearance. The only helmet plates were those worn on occasion by bandsmen. The California saddle with Texas rigging had already replaced the standard cavalry saddle by this date.

B3: Constable, 'scarlet serge', 1878

The scarlet serge tunic, pattern of 1876, was the everyday working tunic for all but fatigue duties. The carbine is the '76 Winchester with a long

forestock and nosecap, introduced in 1878 to replace the single-shot Snider Enfield. In summer the dark blue pillbox cap with a yellow band replaced the fur winter cap. Tunic and breeches were worn tight and close-fitting.

Background: Fort Walsh, headquarters of the Force 1878–82, was abandoned in 1883, but rebuilt as a remount stud ranch in 1943. The original buildings were reproduced, and are today preserved as a national historic site by Parks Canada.

C1: Staff sergeant, full dress, 1886

The full dress introduced for senior NCOs in 1882; based on a photograph of William Parker. The pouch belt supported a black leather binocular pouch with brass monogram; the white cross strap supports the haversack. By this date NCOs carried the 1822 pattern British cavalry sword. Chevrons, worn here above the Austrian knot, sometimes had the knot superimposed. Note North West Canada Medal for service in the 1885 rebellion, with bar 'Saskatchewan'.

C2: Superintendent, undress, 1890

The British cavalry pattern undress tunic was adopted in 1886, as was the Field Service cap with embroidered badge. If parading with constables in full dress, officers wore the white helmet with this tunic.

C3: Sergeant Major, undress, 1890

The dark blue senior NCOs' undress tunic was adopted in c.1886, although the scarlet serge was also retained. Note cloth-covered button securing end of cap 'bag'.

Background: The Riding School, Depot Division, Regina was built in 1888, and destroyed in a spectacular fire in 1920. It greatly improved mounted training, which could now be carried out in all weathers.

D1: Superintendent, full dress, 1886

The British Army dragoon-pattern tunic was adopted in this year. Brown leather pouch belt, waist belt and sword slings were introduced as an

White linen haversack belonging to Reg.No. 2671 Const. Michael Schaab, NWMP. Introduced in 1876 and in use until 1903 as part of full dress uniform, this very practical item was worn with all orders of dress, on parade or patrol. (Glenbow Museum)

economy measure, but were unpopular, and were relegated to undress use in 1890. The black leather binocular pouch was worn in place of the embroidered pouch. No badge was worn on the helmet.

D2: Inspector, full dress, 1910
The gold lace pouch belt, waist belt and sword slings with purple 'lights' were introduced in 1890; rank badges were transferred to the shoulder cords in 1903, and the collar and cuffs became dark blue with the designation 'Royal' in 1904. Collar badges also appeared in 1903. By 1910 the 1908 pattern cavalry sword was in use. Note gilt badge on helmet.

D3: Constable, patrol dress, 1890
The brown cotton duck working uniform worn for fatigues and patrols had been in use for some years; it gradually evolved into a smart, tailored garment, while remaining more practical for rough travel than the scarlet serge. The 'deerstalker'-style cap was a practical innovation, giving some shade to the eyes, though hardly elegant. Note long stirrup length of the California saddle, and the horn to which the carbine was attached.
Background: The Commanding Officer's House at Fort Battleford, 1885; a substantial house in the Gothic Revival style, it still stands today at Fort Battleford national historic park.

E1: Constable, Golden Jubilee, 1897
The scarlet serge undress tunic and newly introduced Stetson hat were worn—rather than full dress—in Queen Victoria's Golden Jubilee parade; and created a striking image of a practical, down-to-earth body of men in contrast to the exaggerated finery of some of the other troops taking part. Note '76 Winchester carbine and bandolier of 45/75 cartridges.

E2: Constable, full dress, 1910
The dark blue gorget patches had indicated the 'Royal' designation since 1904. The cavalry pattern bandolier carries ammunition for the new Lee Metford carbine; a waterproof coat was carried behind the saddle, a valise containing the pea-jacket in front.

E3: Veterinary Surgeon, Service Order, 1904
Only surgeons at Headquarters wore the special coloured cap bands. Note the newly introduced Sam Browne equipment, and the 1896 pattern British cavalry sword.
Background: NWMP post at Dawson City in the Klondike, 1902. Log buildings like this—substantial and practical, but offering spartan comfort—were erected by the Force throughout the prairies and the Yukon.

F1: Assistant Commissioner, full dress, 1930
Commissioners and Assistant Commissioners wore the cocked hat with full dress—with 8 in. and 6 in. plumes respectively—during the 1930s, when the

Sketch of NWMP constable's kit layout plan, 1884. A considerable amount of kit had to be accounted for at inspection, including the horse's bridle. Missing from this layout are the 'scarlet serge', pillbox cap, revolver holster and belt, presumably being worn for the inspection. Barrack beds at this date were wooden boards laid on two trestles. (RCMP Museum)

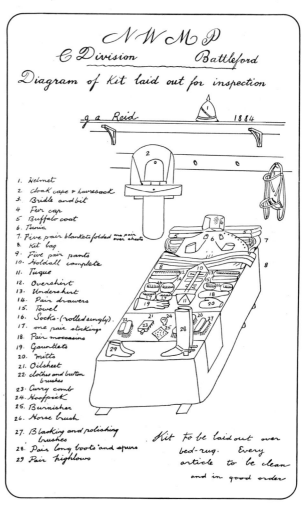

NWMP
C Division   Battleford
Diagram of Kit laid out for inspection

g a Reid   1884

1. Helmet
2. Cloak cape & haversack
3. Bridle and bit
4. Fur cap
5. Buffalo coat
6. Tunic
7. Five pair blankets folded in pair over sheets
8. Kit bag
9. Five pair pants
10. Holdall complete
11. Tuque
12. Overshirt
13. Undershirt
14. Pair drawers
15. Towel
16. Socks (rolled singly)
17. one pair stockings
18. Pair moccasins
19. Gauntlets
20. mitts
21. Oilsheet
22. clothes and button brushes
23. Curry comb
24. Hoofpick
25. Burnisher
26. Horse brush
27. Blacking and polishing brushes
28. Pair long boots and spurs
29. Pair highlows

Kit to be laid out over bed-rug. Every article to be clean and in good order

Pillbox cap decoration in gold braid and lace: these caps are those shown in Plates A3 (top) and B1 (bottom).

Helmet with RCMP badge worn by former members of the Dominion Police after amalgamation with RCMP in 1920; they continued to wear their blue uniforms in Ottawa until the early 1930s, when they adopted regulation RCMP scarlet. (RCMP Museum)

1890 uniform reached its apogee. By the 1942 Regulations it was optional, and the peaked cap and 'scarlet serge' could be worn alternatively. Note 1896 pattern sword still worn by this officer, based on a photograph of Asst. Comm. Worsley, who had commanded 'B' Sqn. RNWMP in Siberia. For this campaign he was awarded the Japanese Order of the Rising Sun, which he wears here with the British War and Victory medals.

F2: Trooper, 'B' Sqn. RNWMP; Siberia 1919
The unit wore standard Canadian Army mounted troops' khaki uniform, with RNWMP collar and cap badges; note Corps sleeve patch. 1908 pattern other ranks' cavalry swords were carried, the guards painted khaki-brown.

F3: Sergeant, No. 1 Provost Company; England, 1942
Regulation Canadian pattern khaki battledress was worn, with the RCMP badge backed red on the FS cap, RCMP shoulder titles, a Military Police brassard just below the right elbow, and the sleeve patch of 1 Canadian Infantry Division.

Details: Top—RCMP plate worn on blue helmet by 'A' Division, Ottawa, which consisted mainly of men absorbed from the Dominion Police in 1920. Bottom—RNWMP brass cap badge, 1910.

G1: Superintendent, full dress, 1967
Officers have dark blue collars and cuffs, while other ranks have dark blue gorget patches only. Plaited shoulder cords were detachable from the dark blue cloth shoulder straps. This is the tunic known today as the 'scarlet serge'. Full dress is still worn today, but restricted to very 'high profile' ceremonial occasions. The 1908 pattern cavalry officer's sword is always worn with the knot unwrapped.

G2: Superintendent, Review Order, 1967
Worn by officers when parading with other ranks in full dress; this uniform is still regulation, but is seen less and less frequently. Note cavalry pattern Sam Browne with whistle. Obscured here, the spurs have chains beneath the instep.

G3: Superintendent, Mess Kit, 1967
Still worn today for formal evening social occasions;

out of doors the peaked cap would also be worn. Miniature decorations, if awarded, are worn on the left lapel above the collar badge.

Background: Left—guidon of RCMP with battle honours 'North West Canada 1885', 'South Africa 1900–02', 'Siberia 1919', 'France & Flanders 1918' and 'Europe 1939–45'. Right—badge of the RCMP in full heraldic colours.

H1: Constable, Service Order, 1960
The everyday brown working uniform, often worn with the peaked cap and the yellow-striped dark blue trousers, as seen today. Note blue piping edging the brown shoulder straps.

(1) **Brass snake clasp with raised 'MP' worn on the leather belt used with the Norfolk jacket, 1874. (2) NWMP officer's belt plate, worn under the 1876 pattern tunics: gilt with silver buffalo head, dark red leather belt with gold stripes. Worn after 1886 with, first, the plain leather belt, and later the gold-laced belt with purple 'light' until 1904, when 'Royal' was added to the inscription. Other ranks wore a plain snake** buckle without the 'MP' until the introduction of Sam Browne equipment, 1903. (3) RCMP officer's belt plate, all gilt, worn from 1920 until at least 1939. (4) RCMP officer's full dress gilt belt plate worn with modified full dress post-1945, with the gold and purple belt; currently worn with Queen's crown motif. (5) Officer's sword sling buckle, gilt, 1886–1939. (6) Officer's sword sling buckle, post-1945.

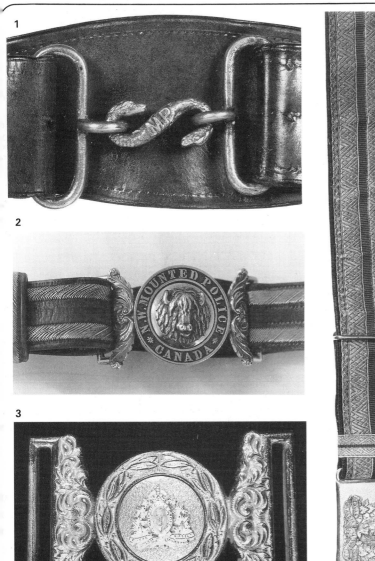

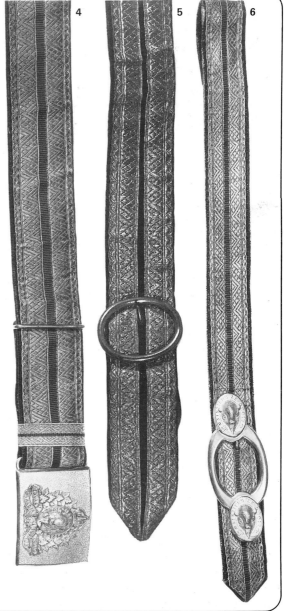

H2: Female constable, full dress, 1987

Devised to retain the distinctive colours and insignia while presenting an appearance appropriate for women members of the Force. Rifle and pistol marksmanship badges, and a star for each five years' service, are worn on the left sleeve only, as on male uniforms.

H3: Constable, full dress, 1987

Known in the Force as 'Review Order', this is worn on ceremonial occasions and special parades. Left sleeve insignia, where applicable, are worn as in H2. The shoulder title is 'GRC' in an arc over 'RCMP' in a line. The holster is worn on the right side of the Sam Browne, with a combined case for six cartridges and handcuffs on the left.

Background: Helicopters and sea-going boats are among the modern methods of transportation widely used by the Force today.

* * *

This has been, necessarily, a much condensed account of the history and the uniforms of the Royal Canadian Mounted Police; and interested readers are referred to the following bibliography for further reading:

Bibliography & Further Reading:

Goldring, Phillip *The First Contingent NWMP 1873–74*; Canadian Historic Sites Occasional Papers in Archaeology & History No. 21; Parks Canada, Ottawa

(1) 1876 pattern officer's sabretache badge, gilt with silver buffalo head; a smaller version was worn on the undress pouch. Neither officers nor other ranks wore helmet plates until after 1904. (2) 'ERVII' brass NWMP cap badge, 1901–04, after which 'Royal' was added to the scroll. Collar badges were a smaller version, in blackened silver for Field Service and fatigue tunics. At this time officers wore embroidered cap badges. (3) 'GRVI' brass RCMP cap badge. (4) 'EIIR' brass RCMP cap badge in use since 1952; note that since 1912 an 'S' has been added to the previously incorrect spelling 'MAINTIEN' in the motto. (5) Current badge, gilt with black enamel backing to the lettering and red to the crown. (RCMP)

Horrall, S. W. *The Pictorial History of the Mounted Police 1873–1973*; McGraw-Hill Ryerson, Toronto, 1973

McCullough, A. B. *Papers relating to the North-West Mounted Police and Fort Walsh*; Manuscript Report No. 213; Parks Canada, 1977

McLeod, R. C. *The NWMP & Law Enforcement 1873–1905*; University of Toronto Press; Toronto, 1976

Morgan, Edwin Charles *North West Mounted Police 1873–1883*; Parks Canada Manuscript No. 113, 1970.

Morrison, William R. *Showing the Flag. The Mounted Police and Canadian Sovereignty in the North 1894–1925*; University of British Columbia Press, Vancouver, 1985

Nevitt, R. B. (ed. Hugh A. Dempsey). *A winter at Fort Macleod*; Glenbow Alberta Institute, Calgary, 1974

Parker, William (ed. Hugh A. Dempsey). *William Parker Mounted Policeman*; Glenbow-Alberta Institute, Calgary & Hurtig Publishers, Edmonton, 1973

Phillips, Roger F. & Klancher, Donald J. *Arms & Accoutrements of the Mounted Police 1873–1973*; Museum Restoration Service, Bloomfield, Ont. 1982

Public Archives of Canada. *Record Group 18. Royal Canadian Mounted Police*; Correspondence, Orders, Dress Regulations, Official Journals etc from 1873 to the present

Reports of the Commissioner 1874–1881; Ottawa; MacLean, Roger & Co. Facsimile edition 'Opening up the West'; Toronto 1973, Coles Publishing Co.

Reports of the Commissioner 1886–1887; Ottawa; MacLean, Roger & Co. Facsimile Edition, 'Law & Order'; Toronto 1973, Coles Publishing Co.

Reports of the Commissioner 1888–1889; Ottawa; Queen's Printer. Facsimile Edition, 'The New West'; Toronto, 1973, Coles Publishing Co.

Ross, David *Uniforms of the NWMP*; RCMP Quarterly, Summer 1980.

Ross, David *Two NWM Police Uniforms 1879*; Journal of the Society for Army Historical Research, Vol. XLVIII, No. 194. London 1970

Ross, David *Uniforms of the North West Mounted Police 1873–1885*; A manual for Guides, Parks Canada, Winnipeg, 1987

RCMP blue Service Order uniform for senior NCOs, *c.*1960: forage cap with yellow band; King's crown cap badge but Queen's crown collar badges—a sometimes condoned irregularity; staff sergeant's gold chevrons with gold Rough Rider badge; brass buttons; officer's pattern Sam Browne. (Glenbow Museum)

Steele, Samuel B. *Forty Years in Canada*; McClelland, Goodchild & Stewart, Toronto, 1914. Facsimile Edition 1972, McGraw-Hill Ryerson, Toronto

Turner, John Peter *The North West Mounted Police*; 2 vols. King's Printer, Ottawa, 1950

(Parks Canada publications are available on inter-library loan from Provincial Libraries or Parks Canada Libraries.)

Notes sur les planches en couleur

A1: D'après une photographie d'époque de l'agent de police Hare et la veste qui a été préservée, dite du 'Norfolk' du chef de police Crozier—notez son col bleu. Il semble que les pantalons distribués aient été au hasard ocres, gris, blancs ou bleus. L'on portait un ceinturon de cuir et un étui de révolver pendant le service. **A2:** Tenue d'officier complète dont le modèle est de 1876, d'après une photographie du célèbre *Sam Steele*; les couleurs sont écarlate et or selon le style des hussards britannique, casque blanc de service à l'étranger avec plumet ajouté. **A3:** Tenue de service quotidienne; à la ceinture portant la cartouchière était aussi accroché un étui à jumelles avec écusson doré. *Arrière-plan*: le Lower Fort Garry.

B1: La tunique de l'uniforme complet de 1876 se portait accompagnée de la toque plate en petite tenue. Les chevrons qui officiellement devaient se porter sur le bras droit uniquement apparaissent sur les deux sur certaines photos. Notez l'épée dont le modèle date de 1853. **B2:** Tenue complète d'agent de police—y compris le havresac roulé—qui a peu changé entre 1876 et 1903. La selle est celle nommée '*California stock*' avec le '*Texas rigging*'. **B3:** Cette tunique est l'uniforme quotidien surnommé le '*scarlet serge*' (serge écarlate), avec képi en fourrure pour l'hiver et toque plate en été. La '*76 Winchester*' pour fusil. *Arrière-plan*: le Fort Walsh.

C1: Tenue complète des anciens sous-officiers, modèle de 1882; le noeud autrichien se portait sur le revers de la manche pouvait se superposer aux chevrons ou ils pouvaient se placer séparément. Sur le ceinturon portant la cartouchière est suspendu un étui à jumelles noir avec monogramme de laiton tandis que sur la bandoulière blanche est accroché le havresac. Les sous-officiers portaient alors l'épée dont le modèle date de 1822. **C2:** Tunique de petite tenue de la cavalerie britannique adoptée en 1886—de même que le calot de service en campagne avec écusson brodé pour les officiers. **C3:** Tunique de petite tenue, bleue sombre, adoptée par les anciens sous-officiers vers 1886, quoique l'on ait aussi conservé la '*scarlet serge*'. *Arrière-plan*: Centre d'instruction de cavalerie, le dépôt Regina.

D1: Tunique dont le modèle est celui des dragons, adoptée en 1886; la buffleterie de cuir uni qui fut introduite par mesure d'économie, n'était pas populaire et fut conservée pour la petite tenue après 1890. **D2:** Les ceinturons à lanières pourpres et dorées de cuir furent adoptés en 1890; en 1903 les insignes de rang portés sur le col furent déplacés sur l'épaule; en 1904, le col et les revers de manche devinrent bleus pour les officiers, avec la désignation '*Royal*'. **D3:** Uniforme de corvée de coton brun, porté ici avec un curieux 'chapeau de chasse'; cette tenue s'est transformée en une élégante tunique de service au cours des années. *Arrière-plan*: La demeure du commandant, le Fort Battleford.

E1: Uniforme de petite tenue de serge écarlate porté avec le *Stetson*, en l'honneur du cinquantième anniversaire de la fête du couronnement de la reine Victoria—contrastant par l'élégance du travail avec les plus beaux atours déployés par les autres troupes et qui fit grande sensation sur les spectateurs. Les pantalons serrés et les bottes basses étaient caractéristiques. **E2:** Les pièces cousues bleues foncées sur le col marquaient maintenant le statut 'Royal'; bandoulière, un modèle spécifique de la cavalerie, avec cartouches pour la nouvelle carabine Lee Metford. **E3:** Seuls les chirurgiens portaient dans les quartiers généraux le bandeau couleur cerise sur la nouvelle casquette de petite tenue; notez la tunique à quatre poches qui remplaça vers 1904 celle présentée sur C2. *Arrière-plan*: poste du NWMP à Dawson City, dans le Yukon.

F1: Cette tenue complète devint optionnelle sous le réglement de 1942; en alternative, la tunique de 'serge écarlate' et la casquette. **F2:** Les soldats de cavalerie portaient en Sibérie la tenue réglementaire de la cavalerie de l'Armée canadienne avec insignes de col et d'épaule de la RCMP, ce dernier sur la pièce cousue bleue. **F3:** *Battledress* (tenue de combat) réglementaire de l'Armée canadienne avec insignes de la *RCMP* sur le calot et l'épaule, brassard de la police militaire et écusson de la 1ère Division. *Détails*: en haut, écu de casque de la Division 'A', Ottawa, dans les 20er Jahren; en bas, écusson de calot de la RNWMP, 1910.

G1: Les officiers se distinguaient encore par des cols et des revers de manche entièrement bleus foncés. L'aiguillette d'épaule était détachable des pattes d'épaule en toile. La dragonne de cuir de 1908 de l'épée se portait toujours lache. **G2:** Porté par les officiers lors des parades avec les agents de police en tenue complète. **G3:** Dehors la casquette se portait avec cette tenue de mess. *Détails*: à gauche, le guidon de la RCMP avec *battle-honours*; à droite, écusson de la RCMP arborant toutes ses couleurs.

H1: Tenue de service quotidienne, brune. Elle était souvent portée avec une casquette et des pantalons bleus à raies jaunes. **H2:** Uniforme féminin introduit récemment. **H3:** Nommée la '*Review Order*', la tenue complète contemporaine n'est que rarement portée lors des cérémonies. Notez l'insigne 'GRC/RCMP' sur l'épaule dans les deux langues; écussons d'adresse au tir au-dessus des revers de manche; des étoiles—une par quinquennal de service—sur la manche; étui à révolver à droite, et cartouchière/étui à menottes à gauche.

Farbtafeln

A1: Beruhend auf zeitgenössischem Foto von Constable Hare und auf der erhalten gebliebenen. 'Norfolk'-Jacke von Superintendent Crozier—siehe blauen Kragen. Reithosen wurden scheinbar wahllos in Braun, Grau, Weiss oder Blau ausgegeben. Im Dienst wurden Ledergürtel und Halfter getragen. **A2:** Offiziers-Galauniform von 1876, nach einem Foto des aussergewöhnlichen Sam Steele; Scharlach und Gold im britischen Husarenstil, der weisse Auslandsdienst-Helm mit zusätzlichen Rossschwifen. **A3:** Alltagsuniform; der Gürtel m. Taschen trug auch einen schwarzen Fernglasbehälter mit vergoldetem Abzeichen. *Hintergrund*: Lower Fort Garry.

B1: Die Galajacke von 1876 wurde—im Dienst—mit runder Kappe getragen. Dienstabzeichen, offiziell nur am rechten Arm getragen, sieht man auf manchen Fotos an beiden Armen. Siehe Schwert im Stil von 1853. **B2:** Galauniform für Constable—inkl. gerolltem Brotbeutel—zeigte zwischen 1876 und 1903 wenig Änderungen. Der Sattel war ein 'California Stock' mit 'Texas rigging'. **B3:** Diese Jacke ise die sog. 'Scarlet Serge'—Alltagsuniform, mit winterlicher Pelzkappe—im Sommer wurde die runde Kappe getragen. Das Gewehr ist die '76 Winchester'. *Hintergrund*: Fort Walsh.

C1: Galauniform f. Unteroffiziere, Stil von 1882; der österreichische Knoten an der Manschette kann über den Dienstabzeichen liegen, oder auch nicht; Der Gürtel trägt auch eine schwarze Feldstechertasche mit Messingmonogramm, weisse Riemen den Brotbeutel. Unteroffiziere hatten jetzt das Schwert im Stil von 1822. **C2:** Dienstuniform der britischen Kavallerie, übernommen seit 1886—ebenso die feld-kappe—für Offiziere mit gesticktem Abzeichen. **C3:** Dunkelblaue Dienstbluse für Unteroffiziere seit etwa 1886, wenn auch die 'Scarlet Serge' beibehalten wurde. *Hintergrund*: Reitschule, Regina-Lager.

D1: Drachenmusterbluse seit 1886; die glatten Ledergürtel und Schwertgehänge, als Sparmassnahme eingeführt, waren unbeliebt und blieben nach 1890 für die Dienstuniform. **D2:** Gürtel aus violettem Leder und Goldborten wurden 1890 aufgenommen; 1903 wanderten die Rangabzeichen vom Kragen auf die Schulter; Kragen und Manschetten mit der Bezeichnung 'Royal' wurden 1904 für Offiziere blau. **D3** Braune Baumwoll—Dienstuniform, hier mit 'Deerstalker'-Jagdmütze; diese Uniform wurde im Lauf der Jahre zu einer eleganten Dienstbluse. *Hintergrund*: Wohnhaus des Kommandanten, Fort Battleford.

E1: Scarlet Serge-Dienstuniform, mit Stetson, bei der Parade für Königin Viktorias Goldenes Jubiläum—in schlichtem Kontrast zur Eleganz anderer Truppen, was die Zuschauer beeindruckte. Enge Reithosen und niedrige Stiefel waren typisch. **E2:** Dunkelblaue Kragenaufschläge jetzt mit 'Royal'; kavallerieartiges Bandolier mit Patronen für den neuen Lee Metford-Karabiner. **E3:** Nur Ärzte im Hauptquartier trugen das kirschfarbige Band auf der neuen Schirmkappe; siehe Bluse mit vier Taschen, die jene aus C2 etwa 1904 ersetzte. *Hintergrund*: NWMP-Posten in Dawson City, Yukon.

F1: Nach den Bestimmungen von 1942 wurde diese Galauniform zur Option; die Alternative war die Scarlet Serge-Bluse und Schirmkappe. **F2:** In Sibirien trug die Truppe normale kanadische Kavallerieuniform mit RCMP-Kragen und Schulterabzeichen, letztere über dem Corps-Abzeichen. **F3:** Normale Kampfuniform der kanadischen Armee mit RCMP-Kappe und Schulterinsignien, Militärpolizei-Armbinde und Abzeichen der 1. Division. *Details*: oben—Helmabzeichen der A-Division, Ottawa, in den 20er Jahren; unten—RNWMP—Kappenabzeichen, 1910.

G1: Offiziere sind immer noch gekennzeichnet durch dunkelblaue Kragen und Manschetten. Die geflochtenen Schnüre der Epauletten sind von diesen abnehmbar. Die Lederschlinge des Schwerts von 1908 wird immer lose getragen. **G2:** Getragen von Offizieren bei Parade mit Constables in Galauniform. **G3:** Im Freien wurde die Schirmkappe mit der Messuniform getragen. *Details*: links—RCMP-Standarte mit Gefechtsauszeichnungen; rechts—RCMP-Abzeichen, vollfarbig.

H1: Braune Alltagsuniform, oft mit Schirmkappe und blauen, gelbgestreiften Hosen getragen. **H2:** Die kürzlich eingeführte Uniform für Frauen. **H3:** Die heutige Galauniform, als 'Review Order' bekannt, wird nur selten bei sehr feierlichen Anlässen getragen. Siehe zweisprachige 'GRC/RCMP'-Schulterinsignien; Scharfschützenabzeichen über der Manschette; Sterne—je einer für 5 Jahre Dienst—am Ärmel; Halfter auf der rechten und Patronen/Handschellentasche auf der linken Seite.